ADOPTED – ME?

ADOPTED – ME?

So Who Do I Think I Am?

To Peter & Carol
best wishes
John

John Thompson

authorHOUSE®

AuthorHouse™ UK Ltd.
1663 Liberty Drive
Bloomington, IN 47403 USA
www.authorhouse.co.uk
Phone: 0800.197.4150

First published in Great Britain in 2013 by Authorhouse UK

Published by AuthorHouse   06/06/2013

ISBN: 978-1-4817-9472-5 (sc)
ISBN: 978-1-4817-9473-2 (hc)
ISBN: 978-1-4817-9474-9 (e)

CONTENTS

Acknowledgements

One evening in October 2002 whilst having dinner with a golfing partner in Le Petit Normand, a small bistro restaurant in Bayeux in northern France, we started up a conversation with the two adjacent diners. We learned they were called Jeff and Laura, and they were on a European tour, visiting from the United States.

During coffee, I talked with Laura, an advertising executive from New Jersey who wrote children's books as a hobby, about my desire to write an autobiography. I told her it would highlight my adoption and subsequent life. After hearing a brief resume of my experiences, she told me not to hesitate and to write it from the heart. I have tried to do this. As we parted, I said I was born John Thompson, and she exclaimed, "Good heavens, my father's name is also John Thompson!" This is just one of many coincidences that occurred during the lead-in to writing my story. I hope you will enjoy reading this book. I thank Laura for all of her positive advice that evening.

My gratitude goes to my wife, Jill, for all her loving encouragement, devotion, patient listening, and hours of proofreading and IT advice during the making of this book. I give grateful thanks to Carolynn, David, Sally, and Tim for their individual sterling efforts, editing advice, and recollections of the past.

I would also like to thank Colin and Kate Gundry for their patience in collating the photographs and illustrations from their UK Southampton Studio, entityphotographic.com.

My grateful thanks go to family members for the many photographs included. The photograph of St James Church, Sutton Cheney by courtesy of the late Roy Illston. Internal and external photographs of Shenton Hall by kind permission of Knight Frank International at Stratford upon

Avon, Warwickshire and Map of Bosworth Battlefield by courtesy of John Nichols.

Lastly, but also of great importance, huge thanks to the editorial and support staff at Authorhouse UK for their skills in the final stages of editing, the design and publishing of my book.

PREFACE

This story is about family trauma that started over thirty years ago. This trauma was made up of a stressful and acrimonious divorce, including a custody battle for two children, during which, at the age of 43, I found out that I had been adopted as a baby; I was a love-child from the 1930s. This was followed by a lengthy but successful search for my natural mother, which led me to a sister, and over time I also found a brother, two more brothers and, finally, a father. I uncovered my family history going back over seven hundred years, including some who were high-ranking officials of the Church of England, in the 1500-1600s. Finally, after two broken marriages and several romantic relationships, I achieved marital bliss.

Life's journey can be very complicated. I have tried to set out how much love and gratitude I owe to my four loving parents—the two parents who adopted me at birth and who I believed were my actual parents for forty-three years and my two natural parents, who I came to know and love after I found them. It has been a cathartic and emotional experience to record the events of this journey. My recollections are based mostly on brief diary notes and letters on file that have brought my dormant memory slowly back to life. My story includes several lucky breaks and many coincidences along the way.

– 1 –

ADOPTION TRAUMA

Although my story begins more than thirty years ago, in 1979, I can still recall the event quite clearly. I stood by the window at home, overlooking the garden of our modest, detached house on the edge of Surrey's leafy suburban belt on a grey, September Saturday morning. I was talking to my parents on the telephone about a letter that they had received from my first wife stating that providing the financial arrangements of the divorce were satisfactory, she would now agree to the children living with me. This was a considerable concession and breakthrough on the stalemate position of our separation, which had been going on for nearly two years.

I had already received from my parents a copy of my wife's letter, but my solicitor said that it would not stand up in court, so he needed to see the original letter. I repeatedly gave this message to my parents on the telephone that morning, but they were very hesitant because of a dreadful thing mentioned in the letter, which they had blanked out in the copy they sent me. I replied that a few more dreadful words would not make any difference.

My parents said that it was really not possible to send the original letter, but I continued to press them to do so. I knew it could bring about a resolution to my separation and put an end to the constant stressful arguments that were affecting the children. Dad asked me to wait for a few moments so he and Mum could discuss the matter together. My father returned to the phone and said he had some very serious news to tell me that was included in the part of the letter they had blanked out. He said, "I have to tell you that we adopted you when you were a small baby." I reacted with utter shock, surprise, and dismay that at the age of 43, I had not known that I was adopted, although it seemed half the close family did. My mother was in tears and couldn't speak. My father ended the conversation by saying how sorry he was.

I was devastated by this bombshell and could hardly comprehend that my wife, after nineteen years of marriage and occasional contact through our childhood, as our parents were close friends, had known for all those years that I was adopted. It was many years later that I learnt the full truth of the accidental leakage of this family secret. When my wife was about 14 years old, she accidentally overheard a conversation between her parents about my adoption. Later, she asked her mother about it and was told never, ever, to mention it again to anyone.

My mother-in-law, who was also my godmother, was horrified that her daughter should have disclosed this secret at such an insensitive time. I was angry and upset, as were my adoptive parents at being forced into disclosing their secret. At the time, during the divorce, very derogatory remarks were made to me about my adoptive parents for not telling me and about the probable slum origins of my natural mother.

My wife and I both adored our two children, and she was a very loving and caring mother, but we didn't always seem to work as a family unit. When the children were both at nursery school, my wife had a very serious car accident that was the other driver's fault. She was very badly injured, and it was several years before she could resume a fairly normal life. During part of this period, whilst caring for my wife, I was virtually both father and mother to our two children, with help from family and close friends. To cope with this sudden family calamity, I had to ask my wife's sister to look after our lovely 3 year old Labrador, with whom she stayed sadly, for the rest of her life.

Our marriage was a very happy one to start with, but as the children were growing up, my wife became unhappy with my modest income and frustrated that she couldn't follow her career whilst caring for our children. Always under pressure for us to move to a larger and more expensive house and, in an attempt to do this, I was encouraged to change my employer, which I did five times in eleven years. The relationship became strained, and we gradually grew apart, which encouraged a climate of confrontation over many years. When I said I wished to start a new life, she insisted that the children should live with her and that I should vacate the matrimonial home.

Our children expressed the wish to live with me, but my wife disagreed and told them in very strong terms that they would not be able to live with their father after I moved out, to the gradual detriment of her relationship with them. At the beginning of the separation they were 11 and 12, and even threatened to run away rather than live with their mother. After work, I would often come home to find my wife angry, resentful, and furious that I was still living there; this tension went on for nearly two years, as I would not give up on the children or leave home.

In view of this awful stalemate within the divorce proceedings, a social services counsellor was appointed by the courts to investigate the family and prepare a report for the judge. The counsellor advised at the beginning of this process that she would be interviewing all four of us in the family separately and that normally it would take about four to six weeks before a recommendation could be made. Ours took eight weeks. The children were questioned and asked to draw pictures of their family.

I was warned by various friends and my solicitor that the chances of the children being allowed to live with their working father were slim and unprecedented. However, eventually the courts ruled in favour of our children living with me, and my wife moved to live locally and continue her career. Some weeks later at a follow up meeting, social services, who I must say were extremely kind in the handling of our case, advised me that at one stage they had considered putting both children into care. Thank goodness that didn't happen. I regret the upset to the children and close family that occurred, but I thought it was the right thing to do at the time.

I gradually adjusted to the life of a single parent with two teenage children and put any future personal life on hold. I advertised for a local surrogate grandmother to be in the house when they came home from school and to cook them a meal and tackle the ironing and a little housework. This worked very well until they grew older and were able to look after themselves. According to their school teachers, my children hadn't shown any changes in behaviour during the years during and following the divorce, but later, my daughter felt the full effects of the marriage breakdown, and she resorted to regular counselling.

After some months, I gradually persuaded the children to visit their mother with me, and much later, we all occasionally had Sunday lunch together. For several years, we all spent Christmas together, with our close relatives. This resulted in a quieter time of reconciliation for the children.

I was fortunate to have a considerate managing director as my boss at the Wembley Stadium Complex, who allowed me flexible working hours.

During the two years after I received the bombshell news from my adoptive parents, I thought about it a great deal. The news of my adoption forms a fundamental beginning to this book and was pivotal to me starting a search for my natural parents. It raised questions in my mind as to why my natural mother had me adopted. However, I had always been rather puzzled by how my traits and aspirations were so different from my adoptive parents. This led to an increasing curiosity which eventually got the better of me. Although shocked, I put to one side the wicked rumour about my natural mother's alleged seedy occupation in Wolverhampton that emerged during the tensions of the divorce and decided that I might try and trace her. I believed I only needed to know if she, or indeed my father, was still alive and a few other basic facts, and then I would take it no further. I thought, *Of course, by now they may have already passed away, and perhaps the search will be futile.*

Following the sudden disclosure of my adoption, my father sent me the original adoption order, stamped by the Clerk of the Justices, County of Kent, Bromley Division, dated 7 December 1937. It included my natural mother's name, Marjorie Irene Thompson, but no address and stated that I, John Thompson, was born in Wolverhampton on 3 July 1936, but I had been renamed Brian Ernest Hughes. The legal costs to adopt me were thirteen shillings and three pence! In addition, my father gave me a certified copy of an entry in the Adopted Children Register at Somerset House, London, with my adopted name, Brian Ernest Hughes, dated 5 January 1938, eighteen months after I was born. I had not, of course, seen either of these two documents before.

I had always had a birth certificate in that name and date of birth, but it was dated 12 February 1949 and was devoid of all parent names and addresses. I can only assume that my parents, in perhaps trying to protect my feelings, never wanted me to know about my adoption or for me to see my original birth certificate, as that specified my previous name and natural mother, so they had a shortened version made for me in 1949. I did not question the thirteen years' difference between this form and my birth date; I accepted it as normal during those post-World War II days.

I did, however, sometimes question in my youth why I was so different physically from my parents. They were rather portly, and I was very slim and tall for my age. In the end, I put it down to being like my maternal grandparents. I learnt many years later, after the adoption news had been broken to me, that discussions had taken place among close relations to tell me that I was adopted, but the idea was abandoned; I can't remember why.

The year of 1936 was, for the British royal family, a turbulent and challenging year. George V died in January, having reigned for twenty-five years. He was followed by his son, the then Prince of Wales, who became Edward VIII. He reigned until December of that year before abdicating to marry an American divorcee. His brother, George VI, ascended to the throne and reigned until his untimely death in 1952.

In 1936, the Summer Olympics were held in Berlin in Germany; this was three years before the outbreak of World War II in 1939. It was an uncertain and troubling time for many families throughout Europe and beyond, including, as I found out, my own family.

– 2 –

DECISION TO SEEK MY NATURAL MOTHER

Sometime during the late summer of 1981, after a couple of years considering the shock of my adoption and the daunting nature of the prospect, I made up my mind to search for my natural mother. It was not an easy decision; on the one hand, there were the awful rumours that she was probably a prostitute, as mentioned in the previous chapter. On the other hand, I had my adoptive parents' feelings to consider. They had been criticised by my wife—their goddaughter and daughter-in-law. Perhaps my ex-wife had miscalculated that my Solicitor would call for the original letter, and she thought my parents wouldn't have the courage to tell me. I heard that she hoped it would all come out at the Divorce Court hearing and force me to capitulate in shame over my illegitimacy, which even by the late 1960's, was considered a social stigma.

Churchill once said the truth can be protected by deception or, put another way, a bodyguard of lies. In light of this idea, who should judge the reasons my adoptive parents had in keeping their secret for so many years? Were they protecting my feelings on the matter? Or did they intend to create a shield of love, perhaps? I hold no grudge whatsoever at their desire to keep this adoption a secret. Perhaps they were trying also to protect my natural parents from the embarrassment of disclosure.

With considerable trepidation, I commenced my search, on the telephone, with St Catherine's House, Kingsway, London. They suggested I should contact the General Register Office at Somerset House, also in London; they also advised me to contact the social services department at the City of Westminster, which I did. I was told it was most unlikely that records of an adoption during the mid-1930s would have survived World War II, due to fire and bomb damage. But the person promised to investigate what records could be found.

Many weeks later, I had a very helpful letter dated 2 October 1981, from the Westminster Social Services Department, stating that my file had been destroyed but enclosing two items.

There was a photocopy of their handwritten index card No.11331/8687A with my birth name, John Thompson, and an address for my natural mother, Miss Marjorie Irene Thompson, Tempsford, Sutton Cheney, Nuneaton.

Beneath this, in typed lettering, was the statement:

> *"Adopted by Mr. and Mrs. E.G. Hughes. Order granted Juv. Court, Bromley, Kent. 7th December 1937."*

This was enclosed with a certified true copy, updated 14 September 1981, of my birth certificate dated 3 July 1936, setting out my mother's occupation as a secretary at a hosiery manufacturing company in Stoke Golding, near Hinckley, Leicestershire. I was apparently born at 74 Tettenhall Road, and my mother's address was given as 99 Tettenhall Road in Wolverhampton. There was no mention of my father on the birth certificate, as was normal in those days.

The adoption order was dated 7 December 1937, so it was clear that I was adopted between twelve and eighteen months old. So, despite Hitler's bomb raids and the Luftwaffe during World War II, some of my documents had survived the Blitz of London! This discovery was an utterly amazing stroke of luck.

In the letter dated 2 October from the Westminster Social Services Department, I was advised that parents who gave their children up for adoption before 1975 believed that their children would never be able to trace them. I was warned it would be quite a shock to an elderly lady, possibly married with a husband and children who knew nothing of her past, to suddenly find a stranger on her doorstep calling her mother. The new Children Act of November 1975 made it possible for children over eighteen to apply for their original birth certificate in an attempt to find their natural parents, but caution was advised.

During this period, I was interviewing paint suppliers and contractors to provide comprehensive tenders for repainting the roof steelwork at the sixty-year-old football Stadium at Wembley. One of the suppliers, Manders Paints Limited of Wolverhampton, was among six contracting firms applying. During one of our meetings, I mentioned to their National Contracts Manager, Bob Jackson, that I was born in Wolverhampton in 1936 and was thinking of trying to trace my natural mother. Bob kindly offered to help me in my search and arranged for me to stay at his house on the outskirts of Wolverhampton. His wife, Kay, who held a senior position in local social services, was extremely supportive and helpful. I couldn't have fallen into safer hands. This was another stroke of luck and possibly the most important pivotal moment in my search.

Early on Monday, 23 November 1981, I set off from home in Surrey for Wolverhampton and met up at 1.30 p.m. with Bob Jackson and spent the evening with him and his wife. The following morning, Bob and I drove to the centre of Wolverhampton to try finding the addresses given on the copy of my original birth certificate: Tettenhall Road, Wolverhampton. After some slow cruising, we found, set back from the road, number 74. It was a small, off-white, two-storey building of considerable age that appeared to be a cottage hospital. We drove into a small car park and, leaving Bob in his car, I walked up the path with some apprehension. I entered the untidy reception area and asked the first person I saw, "Is this building a maternity hospital?" The person, a young carer, looked blank and said she would fetch her manager. I asked the same question and the person replied, "No, but many years ago, it may have been. Now it is a hospice for disabled adults."

This was an important start. Clearly, my natural mother had not resided at number 74, but I could have been born there. So we then looked around for number 99 but could only see a large, new petrol station opposite. We assumed number 99 had been demolished to make way for it. The remaining terraced houses on either side seemed to reflect the era of my birth and earlier.

I thanked Bob for guiding me to the middle of Wolverhampton and said that I would now travel eastwards on my own to find the village of Sutton Cheney in Leicestershire given to me by social services at Westminster. He wished me good luck in my search, pointed me in the right direction for the M6 motorway and I drove south and around the busy north side of Birmingham. I continued along several motorways, before reaching the A5 and headed for Hinckley, finally reaching Stapleton. My pace quickened with excitement when a sign appeared announcing I was approaching Cadeby and Sutton Cheney.

– 3 –

SEARCHING FOR A VILLAGE IN THE MIDDLE OF NOWHERE

After about an hour's drive from Wolverhampton that greyish morning, 24 November 1981, I arrived at Sutton Cheney. It was no more than a hamlet, in a quiet part of rural Leicestershire, in stark contrast to the city I had just left. It consisted of a few pretty cottages, almshouses, a farm called Hall Farm, a village shop and post office, two pubs—The Hercules and The Royal Arms—and a picturesque but ancient village church called St. James. You could easily describe the hamlet as sleepy. I drove up and down the one and only narrow road, looking for a house or cottage called Tempsford. It was like looking for a needle in a haystack. The sensitivity of the search suddenly struck me.

In 1811, John Nichols, a historian, wrote about the village: "To an astonished traveller who has long been spent in populous city, the very hedges were a garden and the meadows and richly cultivated fields a paradise. I can see at this moment the waving corn through which we walked to Sutton Church."

I pulled over and parked the car at the side of the verge and spotted a small post office at the corner of the crossroads. I decided to go inside and look in a telephone directory, but I drew a blank. There was nobody behind the counter; this gave me time to look at the watercolour paintings on the wall, and I discovered that the signature on one of them was R. Thompson. I suddenly felt a ripple of excitement that I was perhaps getting very close to finding more information about my missing mother. Of course, I was ever mindful of the advice of the social services counsellor not to approach her, as it would be an awful shock to her after all those years. A lady from the rear of the post office emerged and asked if she could help me. I said that I was looking for a family by the name of Thompson. She said she did not know of anyone by that name in the village, but I could try in the church. I thanked her and left.

Across the road nestled a beautiful and interesting old church, St James, with a square tower. I approached the church along a flagstone path and asked the person inside the same question: do you know of a family by the name of Thompson in the village? I received the same answer. However, they did suggest that I call and speak to the verger in one of the cottages just past the farm in Main Street, who might have more information. Before I left, I noticed a memorial to King Richard III, who was slain during the battle of Bosworth in 1495, just a few miles away. I hoped that I wouldn't suffer a similar fate by stirring up the past!

Feeling hungry but still excited, I decided to have a lunch and a beer in one of the village pubs. I popped into the Hercules Inn, conveniently opposite the church, thinking it was possibly frequented by some of my family decades ago. Afterwards, feeling more confident that I was at last becoming close to the origins of my family and perhaps my mother, I set off on foot to search for the verger's cottage.

A short walk along the road took me to the verger's cottage. I cautiously tapped on the door, and it opened to a friendly man of mature age. "Come in," he said. "How can I help you?" Despite being a complete stranger, I was shown into a tiny front parlour.

He called his wife, who was hanging out their washing in the back garden, to come and meet me. I explained that I was looking to trace a Marjorie Thompson as part of a search into my family tree. They were both exceedingly kind and spent a long time ruminating about the various families that had lived in the village over the last several decades, but they could not recall anyone by the name of Thompson.

Exhausted of ideas, the verger's wife knocked on the wall intervening with the next cottage and called her sister to come round for a chat. I explained my search, and once again the history of the village was explored over cups of tea as these three people recalled memories further back in time. Suddenly, with a shout, the wife's sister recalled a young woman who lived, for a short time, in the cottage opposite with her aunt and uncle, many years ago, perhaps even before the Second World War. Her name was Marjorie Thompson.

I was overjoyed and suddenly dismayed at the thought that I was so close to possibly finding my natural mother. They all pointed across the road outside the window, and the sister who had remembered my mother said, "That's Tempsford, the cottage you are looking for." The verger went on to say that Marjorie Thompson had married Peter Hall and now lived at Shenton Hall in the next village, called Shenton, a few miles to the west. I was so amazed that my two-day journey to the Midlands had bought forth this much information that I quickly thanked the verger, his wife, and his wife's sister profusely and beat a hasty retreat to prevent disclosing the privacy of the situation about my mother any further. When I got outside, I looked for the Tempsford sign but could not see it on the gate opposite. But it didn't matter. I was getting very close, and the situation was getting more exciting but very scary. I had experienced another stroke of luck!

I turned the car around and set off in the direction of the village of Shenton. I drove through the most beautiful wooded countryside segregated by farmland and then along a very straight road between flat, green fields, passing a sign directing me to the site of the Battle of Bosworth. I saw the various flags for Henry Tudor and King Richard III flying at the top of Ambion Hill, and there was a sign at the next T junction saying "This memorial stone is the spot where it is said Richard III was killed". This location has been subsequently challenged by historians and the memorial stone moved.

Finally arriving in the village of Shenton, I pulled up by the side of another lovely medieval church and went inside. On the floor, much to my amazement, were an assortment of organ parts; the pipes, keyboards, wooden panels, and everything had been stripped out to be reassembled. I asked the man kneeling on the floor if he could direct me to Shenton Hall. "Yes, of course. It's opposite on the other side of the road," he said. So I thanked him, walked out into the bright afternoon sunshine, to look across the road, and was flabbergasted to see a massive Jacobean-style country house. It was surrounded by a boundary wall stretching far away into the distance, both left and right, along the road. It was breathtaking in size, perspective and style.

Was this the birthplace of my forefathers? It was very overwhelming!

I walked nervously across the road and stood at the open gates for several minutes before slowly edging my way forward to get a better look. I stood for ten minutes there, trying to take it all in. The three-sided stable block, with its uneven cobbled yard and wooden doors, were painted blue to match the entrance gates I had just gone through. To the left stood the huge country house with stone mullion windows and ornate red-brick chimneys rising high into the sky.

I was so dumbstruck that I didn't notice a green Range Rover pull into the yard behind me and park on the far side. Oops, I had been told not to approach anyone who may resemble my long-lost mother or other relatives, as they would be hugely shocked. Two middle-aged ladies alighted from the car, one with a large, brown hat, a coloured scarf, and a sheepskin jacket; the other was hatless and less smartly dressed. Had I just stumbled on my natural mother? My mind was exploding, and my heart missed a beat. In my embarrassment, I turned quickly towards the open gate, mumbling my apologies and saying I was currently studying ancient buildings in the area. Fortunately, they ignored me.

I couldn't help comparing what I had just seen with the very modest end-of-terrace, three-bedroom house in Bromley, Kent, where I had been brought up; humble beginnings, indeed, by comparison.

I had no idea at the time who these ladies really were; but, as I hightailed it back to my car and drove off, I excitedly said to myself, "My God! I have just possibly found the home of my natural mother after forty-three years." My elation was tenfold, and I was determined to get back to Surrey as soon as possible and keep my prearranged appointment with the social services counsellor.

I visited Mrs P. Hill at the social services offices at 09.30 on Thursday, 26 November and relayed the detailed events of my journey to the Midlands of the previous two days. *What a coincidence*, I thought. The offices were number 74, the same as the cottage hospital in Wolverhampton. Was this a good omen or not? Mrs Hill expressed surprise at my story and said, "Well, you have almost done my work for me." She said that she would now write to her opposite number in the Midlands and request them to take the search one step further. I was told she couldn't hurry these matters, and requests could sometimes end up with one party or the other wishing not to get involved in any way whatsoever. I was advised to be prepared for this eventuality.

I said to Mrs Hill that I would be quite content with just knowing a few details about my mother and would not press the matter further if that was what she decided.

Sutton Cheney Church, Leicestershire

Shenton Hall front elevation, first seen on my secret visit—1981

Shenton Hall Gatehouse—1981

By comparison my first home, in Bromley, Kent 1937-1960

– 4 –

THE LONG WAIT FOR NEWS

It had been many months since I visited the local social services counsellor, Mrs Hill, in November 1981, but I did make a few phone calls to see how her approach to her opposite number in the Midlands was proceeding. By the spring of the following year, my hopes had diminished and patience lessened. I was concerned that nothing was happening or the trail had gone cold. It was perplexing and frustrating. I wrote to my local counsellor on 1 March 1982 asking if any progress had been made. I received a reply a week later saying that her letter, dated 8 December 1981, had been misdirected to Warwickshire, as my natural mother lived right on the border between Warwickshire and Leicestershire. It had now been redirected to Leicestershire with a request in a follow-up letter from Mrs Hill in early March 1982 for them to act as an intermediary.

I could do nothing but wait. It seemed like an age since my first visit to those quaint villages in Leicestershire the previous November. The months went by into May, June, and July, and still there was no news. My yearnings continued unabated.

In the meantime, I received a very supportive letter from Bob Jackson, my business contact in Wolverhampton, saying how delighted he was that I had managed to trace the village where my natural mother might have lived and inviting me to visit them again.

I was beginning to give up hope when, out of the blue, during the latter part of July, I had a phone call from a Mrs Ann Hall at the social services department in Hinckley, Leicestershire. She said, "The letter sent from Surrey the previous December via Warwickshire eventually reached me in early April." She told me she had asked my mother, also a Mrs Hall, to meet her at the office in Hinckley to discuss a confidential family matter.

My mother was described as a very private lady with a large family, of medium height and build, with fair hair and no glasses; she had not been very well recently. She was prepared to correspond with me and meet up, although she was due to go on holiday on 13 August. I was overjoyed. It had taken eight months to get this wonderful result. At last, would I be able to ask about my forbears, find out more about myself, and establish who I really was? Mrs Ann Hall said, "I suggest you write to your mother using the social services department in Hinckley address."

Here is my letter, word for word, dated 1 August 1982, which I found very difficult to put together.

Dear Mrs Hall,

I was delighted to hear from our intermediary, following my return from holiday, that we shall be able to meet soon, and I'm writing to confirm that I will be extremely happy to meet you either midway or in London, depending upon whether you would prefer to drive or use the train. I would suggest any of the following places:

Stratford upon Avon; Northampton; Milton Keynes; or London, St Pancras station.

Whichever you choose, I shall be happy to agree to, and perhaps we could have lunch. I quite understand your recent feelings of concern at my approach earlier this year, as it also came as a shock to me in 1979 when I found out by accident that I had been adopted. It took me at least a year or more before I decided to begin the search. During this time, I have maintained discretion on this matter and will of course continue to do so by corresponding with Mrs Ann Hall at Trinity Lane.

I look forward very much indeed to hearing from you.

With kind regards,

Yours sincerely,

Brian Ernest Hughes

Several weeks later, a two-page typed reply arrived, dated 23 August, 1982, from my natural mother.

Dear Brian,

Thank you very much for your letter. I was very pleased to get it—I read it several times. I am sorry I have been so long answering it, but I seem to live in a whirl. I have four children, who are married, and I have nine grandchildren. My daughter is separated from her husband, and so I have her two sons quite a lot, aged 10 and 8. They are staying with me at the very moment. Also, my youngest son is having great trouble with his wife, and they have two lovely little girls. His parents-in-law live in the back of their very large house, and now they are all upset, and my son and daughter-in-law need to separate, so really I have been helping to sort that out, but with little success.

It seems a great shame these marriages break up, and I do understand yours has. I did not show your letter to my husband, and that really has caused the delay in me writing to you, but please give me time and I will come and see you somewhere, as you suggest. I tried to ring you all weekend to explain why I had not answered your letter, but it was impossible, so I telephoned this morning and perhaps it was your son who answered the phone. He wanted to give me your office number, but I was not sure if this was a good idea or not.

Anyway, I will get in touch with you again as soon as I can. Can you take a day off in the week, or is this difficult? I'm not sure if you have had all your holidays. I have someone waiting for me to work in the house, so must hurry. I am coming to meet you as soon as I can.

Yours sincerely,

Marjorie Hall

I was over the moon after receiving this letter, and then, some days later at the office, my secretary put through a private call, and a young-sounding female voice said, "Hello, Brian. This is Marjorie Hall."

I just gasped and said "how delighted" and so forth. We talked for a while and agreed we should meet in London, as she was coming up for a theatre matinee the next week. Her train back to Nuneaton departed from Euston, so we could meet under the large clock tower in the station forecourt at 6.00 p.m. on the evening of 2 September. I was so elated that I knew I didn't have to write it in my diary. The date and time were etched in bright colours in my memory. I had been hoping this would happen for months, which turned into years. The last few days, since receiving Mrs Hall's telephone call, I had been thinking about it nonstop, day and night.

Life at the office continued at a hectic pace, with a continuous series of development meetings. I also had teenage children at home to supervise and care for. Here, at last, I was about to meet my natural mother for the first time in my entire life at 46 years of age. My mind was full of questions. What would she be like? Would we get on all right? Would she keep to her promise, or would one of us have an accident that prevented the meeting, as sometimes happens in a film? I had a few doubts but was quietly determined to keep going forward with a strange mixture of excitement and anxiety.

– 5 –

MY ADOPTIVE PARENTS

I was extremely lucky that such loving parents as Mr and Mrs Ernest Hughes adopted me. Dad certainly lived up to his Christian name but was very shy and bordering on reclusive. They were both always very loving and kind to me. My adoptive parents led a very quiet and domesticated life. Dad was educated at Wilson's Grammar School in Dulwich, South London, and was very good at figures and conversational French. He then took a junior position as a local government official in the Rating Office at Southwark Town Hall in London, where he stayed all his life. He rose to be Head of the Department before retiring at 63. Dad was born near the Elephant and Castle in the Old Kent Road and Mum, who was christened Eleanor May, was born in Dulwich. Once married, they lived in Dulwich, where they met and were close friends with my first wife's parents, socialising and playing tennis together.

They moved to Bromley, Kent, in the early 1930s, where they lived for over thirty years and where I spent my childhood and adult years before I was married. My parents eventually retired to a comfortable bungalow in Hailsham, near Eastbourne in Sussex, where Dad took a part-time post as a bookkeeper for a local estate agent until his death in 1983. They enjoyed their retirement by visiting Eastbourne, where they had memories of spending earlier holidays. They ventured on a coach trip, touring many countries in Europe, stopping at many famous cities; Dad refused to fly anywhere by plane, as he preferred his feet on the ground.

They did not spoil me, and they encouraged me to excel in every way at school, the Boy Scouts, the local church choir, the cricket team, and many other pastimes. I was too shy to query why I didn't have any brothers or sisters. Now, I can only assume they were not able to have any children of their own. I did miss not having any brothers or sisters, particularly on holiday, although I didn't know any different. But having school friends in the neighbourhood and participating in a range of hobbies helped to make up for this.

I remember little from my very early years, but photographs show that at the age of three, for best occasion outings, I was smartly dressed in a white satin suit with a matching beret. I learnt from relatives that my parents had doted on me, so much so that when I was a young infant, they wouldn't agree with the local authorities to evacuate me to safer parts of the country to avoid the bombing from the German Luftwaffe during the Blitz. Most neighbours at the time, because of their income level, were allocated either an Anderson metal-framed air-raid shelter for indoors or a concrete block house built in their back garden.

We had neither, due to Dad's salary slightly exceeding the cost of the free-issue scheme. However, neighbours shared their shelter with us every time the sirens sounded, indicating that an air raid was imminent. Bromley in Kent, just outside south-east London, was bombed and damaged but not as badly as central London. Between 1943 and 1945, the German bombing campaign, the V1 flying bombs, and the V2 rockets with their explosive warheads, caused severe damage. They were not advanced enough to land on specific targets; they were launched from secret bases in France and aimed at London on a random basis. Most reached central London; but some fell short by many miles and fell in areas that included Bromley.

As a defence mechanism, London and other cities on their outskirts had a system of barrage balloons. These were large, silver-coloured, cigar-shaped obstructions that floated in the sky, anchored to the ground by steel hawsers and inflated with highly combustible hydrogen gas. They were difficult to see during daylight and caused enemy aircraft to crash or fly off course. At night-time, they were even more devastating and exploded if hit. They were tethered hundreds of feet above-ground when not required; after an air-raid warning, they were floated even higher in the sky.

I recall that our front door was blown in and all the windows smashed when a rocket, or doodlebug, as they were called, landed several hundred yards away. We boys used to spend our time collecting souvenirs of shrapnel pieces of different colours and shapes that had exploded from these rockets and bombs or from aircraft that were damaged as they flew overhead. I also recall seeing plastic blackout sheets at all the house windows to reduce the risk of the Luftwaffe fighter pilots spotting suburban targets.

Despite the War, some years we were able to get away on holiday to the Isle of Wight, Lyme Regis in Devon, or Weymouth in Dorset with its lovely miles of soft yellow sand. I recall being in Lyme Regis around 1943 or '44 when the area was alive with thousands of American servicemen getting ready for the D-Day invasion, or so I realised when I was a lot older. I clearly remember being given delicious American candy, or chocolate, as we know it, when I was restricted to the bedroom with measles in the local bed and breakfast at Up-Lyme, a few miles in from the coast.

Whilst I can remember being argumentative at times, as I disagreed with my parents over a number of issues, overall I had a very happy childhood. Dad encouraged me with stamp collecting, learning chess, fretsaw woodwork, and model aeroplane making; Mum encouraged me with piano lessons and bought me all the current Ivor Novello music albums and sheet music for hit songs of the day. Mum had a lovely soprano voice, and for Christmas and birthdays, the family would gather at her brother's house in Dulwich for a sing-song around their piano. Mum's sister-in-law was a very good pianist, and both Mum and I sang some solo pieces. We all sang in the front room, kept for special occasions. Mum, Dad, and I got to Dulwich from Sundridge Park Bromley by taking a rickety, noisy tram from Grove Park.

When I was eleven or twelve, I had a music teacher called Olive Jones to improve my grades, and I had a crush on her. She was the big sister of one of my school friends, living in Kynaston Road, Bromley. This, conveniently, was on the walk home from school. I was encouraged to join the local choir, and I attended church three times on a Sunday for several years. As head chorister at St Andrew's Church, Burnt Ash Lane, Bromley, I sang solos at weddings for pocket money and took part in special services at Easter and Christmas.

My parents and I lived in a modest, end-of-terrace house near Sundridge Park, Bromley. Mum and Dad, my adoptive parents, bought it soon after they were married in the early 1930s. It had a long, narrow, rear garden with a goldfish pond, a small lawn, flower beds, and a vegetable patch.

My first memory is of a mixed infants' school when I was 5, which would have been in 1941. I recall the vast playground on sandy soil that we were allowed to dig into during playtime, as if we were on the beach, and names of some of the teachers.

When I reached the age of 7 or 8, they separated the boys from the girls for all classes, including separate playgrounds and games areas; this transformed us into a boy's junior school. The state school was in the middle of a large council estate in Downham, located between Bromley and Catford. It catered for boys and girls from 5 to 16, all from very different backgrounds, and there was a strict headmaster, Mr Frederick Yelland, for the boys and a headmistress for the girls. Mr Yelland used to patrol the corridors with cane in hand, looking into the classrooms for any misbehaviour.

My parents were anxious for me to do well, so they entered me, just before the age of 11, for the entrance exam at Eltham College. This was a public boarding school for boys a few miles north of Bromley which took day pupils. Unfortunately, I failed the exam. It may have been a higher standard than the entrance exam for Bromley County Grammar School for which my classmates sat. Indeed, some were successful and progressed to that school. Coaching for exams in those days was limited. I found out more recently that Eltham College, formed in 1842, has a long list of notable Old Elthamians, including the Olympic athlete Eric Liddell.

However, two years later, I passed the entrance exam to Beckenham Technical County School. This school, for three years, gave me an excellent grounding in all basic subjects plus technical drawing. This enabled me to consider a career as an architect or engineer.

The more I write, the more I remember of my childhood, most of which took place more than sixty years ago. I recall being extremely pleased when, after I passed the exams at age 13, in the summer of 1949, my parents—as a complete surprise—bought me a brand new Raleigh Roadster bicycle. It had a Sturmey-Archer three-speed gear hub in blue-and-silver chrome.

I felt like the king of the highway. I was already very keen on cycling, and Dad had a bicycle too. With his encouragement and my new Raleigh Roadster, we both cycled during that summer the twenty-five miles to Westerham and back. On Sunday mornings, we cycled further afield into the Kent countryside, along main roads like Wrotham Hill and country lanes, almost free of car traffic. You could not do that safely today. Very happy days they were.

Dad would sometimes take me with him to watch football at Millwall F. C. on the Isle of Dogs and, on other occasions, to Southwark, Walworth Road Baths, converted in the evening for professional boxing. This was run by the promoter Jack Solomons as a charity event. Tommy Trinder, the famous comedian, raised money via an auction in the interval. Dad was responsible for the box office.

During my last year at school, for one day a week, we were sent to the Bromley College of Arts and Crafts to be taught the basics in plumbing, bricklaying, plastering, metalwork, sign writing, and architectural drawing. This stood me in good stead for studying for architectural exams in the future. It was around this age that I escaped from my parents to share a holiday on a Butlins-style holiday camp on the south coast with my cousins and entered a talent competition, singing Sinatra's "The Lady is a Tramp" and a different ballad I have long forgotten. I thought my mother's enthusiasm for me to learn the piano and sing in the local church choir seemed to have paid off. Unfortunately, the judges did not spot my talent. I was pleased to find I had come sixth, but not when I found out there were only six contestants.

At the age of 16, I sent several application letters to major construction companies and consultants in London. I was fortunate to receive two offers. The first was an offer to be articled to a firm of architects; the second was to start as a junior draughtsman for Sir Robert McAlpine and Sons, in Park Lane, London. I chose the latter, as it offered five shillings a week more. Financial independence came at two pounds and fifteen shillings a week. I slowly pursued a search for fashionable gentlemen's clothes—a sports jacket with side vents, stylish socks and brown suede shoes—and expressed a desire to own a horse. I later bought a white riding mackintosh and said I would like to live in a large, mock Tudor house one day, similar to the one on the main Bromley road. I can't think where these grand ideas came from. My parents, at the time, thought I was just going through a phase, as they didn't have this interest in clothes then, although they did dress fashionably in their young adult years, according to photographs. All these years later, I know why I had this longing and an interest in country pursuits, clothes, especially socks and the countryside in general.

At 17 years old, I decided to apply for national service in the Army. I needed to get away from home. Mum had always been very supportive; but, at times, it was difficult to breathe. I learnt a lot later that Dad had had a very minor indiscretion during Home Guard duties during the Second World War. This may have spoilt their original happy relationship. However, because Dad was a man who disliked social occasions and didn't talk much, Mum leant on me for companionship, for shopping, and as an escort to the cinema through my teens. The older I became, the more embarrassing it was. I would rather have been out with my friends.

Mum even wanted to come with me on the train to the marshalling area in London for all the army recruits, just after my eighteenth birthday, to make sure that I arrived safely and that I got on the right train for North Wales, where I was to be posted. I was sure I didn't need her company, as I had been travelling on the train for work to the offices of Sir Robert McAlpine, at 80 Park Lane, Mayfair, in London, every day for the past two years. Thank goodness Dad persuaded her it wouldn't be a good idea. Can you imagine the Sergeant Major's sarcasm towards me if Dad hadn't been so persuasive?

After three months of basic training at Oswestry in North Wales with the 40th Royal Artillery Field Gun Battery, I was transferred to Larkhill, near Salisbury, to train as a Surveyor RA to locate enemy gun positions. I was selected for officer training leading to Second Lieutenant and passed many levels but failed at the finals. I was asked to reapply later, after further army experience. My posting to Germany was about the most exciting thing that had happened to me so far. It involved a ferry crossing from Harwich to the Hook of Holland, sleeping in the bowels of the ship in a hammock, and a train ride through Holland's characteristically flat countryside, past cheering Dutch children as they spotted our khaki uniforms. Upon reaching Utrecht, then later Arnhem, we entered into

Germany, where our reception was, understandably, very unfriendly. The contrast could not have been greater.

We were eventually driven in a truck to an ex-German-military modern, two-storey barracks at Hohne, between Hamburg to the north and Hannover to the south, in a huge area known as Luneburg Heath. The accommodation was far more comfortable and warmer than the Nissen huts in England. The proximity to the infamous Belsen prison camp loomed in our young minds, and I made a visit there. It was a numbing experience; there was no sign of any wildlife whatsoever, just scorched earth and scrubland. My first leave back to Blighty, as we squaddies used to call it, brought cries from Mum when I uttered a few "bloody this" and "bloody that" in my conversations. She declared, "Oh dear, what has happened to my boy!"

I decided not to reapply for officer training, as I would have had to sign up as a regular soldier for three years, and I was keen to get back to civilian life. I was gradually promoted to full bombardier and then sergeant during my remaining eighteen months in Germany, during which time the gun-locating battery at Hohne was disbanded, and I was transferred along with others to the 45th Field Regiment at Dortmund. This gave me the chance to explore Cologne and the beauty of the Harz Mountains near the border with Soviet Russia. I also took lessons in conversational German whilst in the camp.

By September 1956, back from Germany, I resumed my day and evening studies at Westminster College in London and returned to McAlpine's, the civil engineering contractors in Park Lane. My career from there varied from working with consulting engineers, to design and build contractors, and then property developers, during which period I qualified as a chartered civil engineer. This led me to a project management consultant firm located adjacent to Heathrow Airport, which resulted in a promotion to an associate partner and some very interesting projects to manage.

In 1974 I joined the Wembley Stadium Complex, in north-west London. It was a subsidiary company of British Electric Traction, a large, multinational business conglomerate. I was appointed as the in-house project manager responsible for the successful completion, over a two-year period, of a £23 million construction project at Wembley Stadium. This project comprised the building of the Wembley Conference Centre, a state-of-the-art international conference and exhibition venue, a speculative multistorey office block complex, and extensive coach and car parking that served the entire seventy-acre complex.

I was fortunate to be selected from 150 applicants, perhaps due to my wide range of construction and project management experience and because I had previously worked with a cross section of award-winning design consultants in London.

The Wembley Conference Centre was the first of its size and complexity in the United Kingdom. The centrepiece was an imposing 2,700 seat auditorium, which could revert to a concert hall and became the home of one of the famous London orchestras. It also included audiovisual and multilingual translation facilities for international conferences and exhibitions. As the client lead officer, I was very involved in every aspect of the internal design and external construction, from the complex roof steelwork to the colour of the furnishings and the acoustics of the concert hall.

The conference and exhibition centre was completed on time and within budget. As part of the senior management team, I was introduced to the Duke of Kent at the official opening ceremony in January 1977. Without doubt, this project was the highlight of my career thus far.

I very much enjoyed this exciting career change. By 1981, four years after completion of the new conference and exhibition centre, my contract was extended to supervise a rolling programme of multimillion pound developments on the seventy-acre site. These covered much-needed improvements to Wembley Stadium itself, the adjacent indoor arena, and a new, extended exhibition space.

I was also required to supervise the equipping of the multi-storey speculative office block complex for M.V. Kellogg, a major US international petro-chemical engineering company. This was an additional income stream to support the conference and exhibition centre investment, in parallel to the huge variety of sporting and entertainment events. I was by then on the permanent staff and acting as an executive officer, attending main board meetings in Piccadilly, Mayfair, one of the richest parts of London, chaired by Sir John Spencer Wills. Other notable attendees were Lord De-La Warr, Hugh Dundas, the eminent Architect Richard Seifert, and other BET directors.

Mum & Dad Hughes Wedding early 1930's

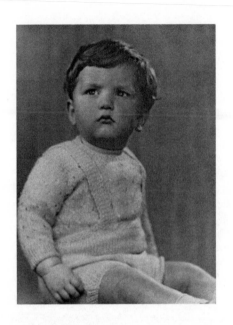

Brian Hughes at 18 months

Brian Hughes at 2 years

Mum & Dad at Eastbourne late 1960's

Royal Artillery- National Service accommodation huts—Oswestry, North Wales

Royal Artillery—hut ready for inspection

Royal Artillery—25 pounder guns on the Parade Ground

Aerial shot of Wembley Stadium Complex—1977

– 6 –

First Meeting with My Natural Mother

The reader will no doubt share with me the mixture of apprehension and excited anticipation leading up to my first meeting with Marjorie Hall, after all that had gone on before; aside from my own research, there was just a very brief description of her by social services and one phone call between us.

We had arranged by telephone to meet at Euston Station at 6.00 p.m. on 2 September 1982, as mentioned previously. That afternoon, I drove down from the Wembley Stadium Complex, where I worked as the estates director at that time.

It was a warm, late-summer evening. I arrived early and parked the car in the side streets and took up a position under the station clock tower. I was very nervous, and my heart was pounding. I didn't have long to wait. At exactly 6.00 p.m., up walked an attractive, well-dressed, elegant lady of middle years. She introduced herself and said, "Hello, Brian. How lovely to meet you," and we warmly shook hands. Such an extraordinary moment, never to be forgotten.

I asked how long we had to talk; her train for Nuneaton didn't leave for about an hour, so we found somewhere in the station bar to sit down and have a drink. Everyone was noisily milling around, totally unaware of the momentous meeting in their midst. I recall that she wore a well-fitted, navy-blue corduroy jacket over a blue-and-cream summer dress with a small, matching navy-blue hat, and she carried a long-handled parasol. She looked as though she had just walked out of Buckingham Palace.

As I write this, some thirty years after that day, it is a highly emotional moment for me, causing me to miss her very much. The reason for this will become clearer later in the book, after reading more of Marjorie Hall's letters to me.

I recall that my mother had just seen *Cats*, the Andrew Lloyd Webber musical, with her son Michael and his Norwegian wife, Eli, who were over from Oslo on holiday. We talked about our different lives; Mrs Hall lived at Shenton Hall with her husband, Peter Hall, who was unaware that she was meeting me. I learnt from my mother a little more about her four grown-up children. I told her about my family, my adoptive parents, and my recent divorce, and I gave her a brief outline of my business career thus far.

This was by far the most extraordinary event in my life. I escorted Mrs Hall to the platform entrance, after we had agreed to continue to write to one another and to arrange for me to visit Shenton in Leicestershire, where she lived. I was thrilled and delighted but couldn't really take in all that we discussed; it all seemed so unreal at the time.

Many months later, my adoptive mother asked if I had made any progress in finding my natural mother. Recognising the sensitivity of the question, I was careful with what I said and just gave her a low-key account of the meeting. I mentioned that I had a stepsister and three stepbrothers living in the Midlands.

I certainly didn't want to hurt her feelings by even hinting at the differences in lifestyle. However, Mum did continue, to her credit, to ask about progress over the years with my other family.

I continued to give her an honest account of developments, whilst having regard to the confidentiality that my natural parents required of me.

– 7 –

FIRST INVITATION TO
SHENTON HALL

The weeks and months continued to pass by at their usual hectic speed, with countless meetings at the office of the Wembley Stadium and Arena Complex with an array of consultants and contractors. Certain evenings and weekends, I had the opportunity to attend some of the various events, such as major sporting cup finals, the FA Cup, international football, and horse shows and pop concerts, like ABBA, Elton John, Queen, Bruce Springsteen, George Michael, and the Live Aid Concert. By this time, my teenage children and their friends were old enough to come by train to Wembley for evening pop concerts, after which I would take them home.

Although I still had my children to look after, thoughts about the extraordinary meeting on 2 September with my natural mother continued to occupy my mind with increasing excitement. We had spoken on the telephone occasionally since our meeting in London, and a date of 20 October was agreed for me to visit Shenton Hall.

I had a postcard from my natural mother dated 11 October 1982 (parentheses mine). It said:

> It was lovely to talk to you on the telephone yesterday, and yes, someone (I presume Mr Peter Hall) did pick up the phone while we were speaking, and at lunchtime I was asked who I was talking to. So I said who it was, and he seemed very interested and said you sounded very nice on the phone and had a voice like a friend of his.

I took Edward and Giles back and met my daughter halfway;* she said the Horse of the Year Show at Wembley Arena was wonderful and that the Atherstone team of children came third. She was with some friends whose daughter was in the team. If the trains to Nuneaton are difficult, then come to Rugby, but of course, Nuneaton is much nearer for me. I will ring you at the weekend to find out what time you arrive. Could you bring some music with you to play? But I do understand if you cannot, and I'm not sure what will be going on in my house that day. I still cannot believe it, and I go from room to room, wondering what I'm doing.

Yours sincerely,

Marjorie Hall.

This was the first of many cards, letters, and telephone calls that we exchanged over the next few years.

*Edward and Giles were the sons of my stepsister, Carolynn, who lived near Rugby.

I decided not to go by train but to use the car for my first visit to Shenton on 20 October. My mother asked me to meet her in the car park at Market Bosworth at 10.00 a.m. To ensure that I was not late, I arranged to stay at a local hotel in Oadby overnight, some fifteen miles away. The following morning, I drove to Market Bosworth and met Mrs Hall as arranged. She then drove me to Shenton Hall and showed me round the lovely, old Jacobean-style country house dating back to the seventeenth century. The rooms were huge, with high ceilings, decorative cornices, magnificent oil paintings, tapestries, antique furniture, and priceless porcelain china dotted about. We had a view of the grounds, which extended to twenty-two acres. There was a walled garden and, beyond the yew topiary hedge, a very large lake surrounded by magnificent ancient trees, several paddocks, and parkland for grazing horses.

Mrs Hall showed me a moulded beam in the kitchen, with these words marked in black: "This hovse was bvilt by me William Wollaston Esq

A.D. 1629." The contrast with the house I grew up in was colossal and rendered me almost speechless.

Later, I saw stabling for half a dozen horses—some containing horses being groomed for fox hunting at the weekend—bales of straw, feed bags, and water buckets. It was almost too much to take in on one day. I recalled my ambition as a teenager to own a horse and decided it was probably in my DNA. I played the grand piano in the drawing room, whilst my mother busied herself around the house.

Over lunch, I learnt that the house had been requisitioned by the War Office during the Second World War and had served as a prisoner-of-war billet for German Luftwaffe prisoners. It was then empty for four years and fell into abject disrepair until Mr and Mrs Hall purchased the property in 1949. Counting all the cellars and attic rooms, together with the old kitchens and staff quarters, the house had nearly one hundred rooms in all, many still in a poor state. She told me it had taken four years to renovate a large part of the property to a habitable standard. Some floors of the west wing, including the original extensive kitchens, remained derelict and out of bounds.

I did not meet my mother's husband, Peter Hall, that day. I was told he was busy at the family business in Hinckley. I plucked up the courage and tentatively asked Mrs Hall if she knew the whereabouts of my father. She turned to me and said, "Darling, if you gave me a thousand pounds, I could not tell you where he is." After this extraordinary day, Mrs Hall drove me back to my car at Market Bosworth, where we said our goodbyes. I promised to return again soon. I decided that, for the moment, I would keep my unauthorised and unannounced visit to Shenton Hall almost a year before to myself.

More than three weeks went by and, for our third meeting, I decided to take Marjorie Hall to a tea dance at the Waldorf Astoria Hotel in the Strand, London, on Friday, 12 November 1982. It turned out to be a particularly momentous day in our relationship, as the reader will discover in the next three paragraphs.

I had taken half a day's leave and left my office at Wembley to meet her at Euston Station at three in the afternoon. We made our way through the heavy traffic to the Waldorf. My mother was in her sixties, and she did not look her age at all. We had a lovely afternoon in the famous Palm Court of this hotel and enjoyed being served with afternoon tea and cakes, interspersed by dancing together to the strains of the four-piece orchestra. At one stage, the leader of the orchestra walked up to us and asked very politely, "Would your wife like a request played for you to dance to." Naturally, we were both a bit taken aback. However, my mother enjoyed that she had been mistaken as my wife rather than my mother. I recall her elegance and easy charm wherever she was or whoever we spoke to that afternoon.

There was more excitement to come. After the dancing had finished and people began to drift away, we drove back to Euston Station. I obtained a platform ticket and walked with my mother to the train. We had to hurry a little, as the train was about to depart. Once inside the carriage, Mrs Hall lowered the window to say her goodbyes. The guard blew his whistle, and suddenly, my mother said excitedly as the train started to pull away, "Brian, you're a Hall!" I began to walk alongside the moving train, not believing what she had said. The train slowly gathered speed, and she waved and smiled at me until the train finally disappeared into the distance.

Driving home, stunned yet again, I was later reminded of the film *Brief Encounter*, in which Trevor Howard stands on the station platform saying goodbye to Celia Johnson as she leans out of the carriage window. As I write this, it brings back many deep emotions, as I miss my mother very much. I did not have very long to enjoy the love and companionship from the mother that I thought I would never meet. Thank God I made the effort to find her before it was too late. I was very fortunate that she lived in Leicestershire all her life and had actually married my father. Oh thank heavens! Had my mother married someone else, would I ever have found her?

Shenton Hall main entrance—A Grade II* Listed Building

Shenton Hall from the lake

Shenton Hall rear elevation

– 8 –

MY NATURAL FATHER
IN DENIAL

Following the revelation by my mother that I was a Hall, she rang me shortly afterwards to beseech me to keep this disclosure a secret. I immediately agreed to her request. I didn't realise until many years later that my father, Peter Hall, upon initially being told about my approach to my mother via social services, was totally opposed to my acceptance into the Hall family. This was seemingly an insurmountable impasse.

He told my mother that he saw nothing but trouble arising from my introduction into the family. He also told my mother vehemently that he would only allow her to meet me providing that on no account could I be told that he was my father. From what I have gleaned since, there must have been many stressful arguments behind closed doors during the years following my appearance. There is little doubt that these disagreements were to the detriment of my mother's health. Father wanted me banned, and Mother wanted me to gradually become part of the family.

Looking back now, I understand that Father didn't really know me from Adam. He was extremely wary of encouraging a complete stranger into his family of competitive sons. For all he knew, I might have had millions of pounds in inherited wealth from somewhere and could make hostile bids for his company. Of course, nothing was further from the truth. All I wanted was, at long last, to belong to the family of my origin and to settle in my mind once and for all the answer to the question, who do I think I am?

Marjorie wrote to me on 15 November 1982, the following Monday, a nine-page confidential letter about her childhood and teenage years and the stressful life with the Halls. Here is a very short extract, followed by a longer summary of her earlier years, taken partly from this letter and partly from my own assessment of what probably happened to her between 1935 and 1936, when I was conceived and later born. There is no doubt that she was so traumatised during this period that she was unable to consign her experiences to paper or talk to me in about it detail.

My Dearest Brian,

Thank you for such a happy time with you dancing at the Waldorf—it was the happiest day I have ever spent. I'm sorry I told you the news as the train left the station, but when I looked at you and knew I had not told you the truth, then I realised that you must know. If Peter knows I have told you, he will kill me.

Don't forget, I love you. See you very soon.

Marjorie

In 1981, about a year before we met, Marjorie had already been diagnosed with temporal arteritis. This is an inflammation of the arteries in the head, strongly associated with polymyalgia rheumatica, called PMR. The standard treatment with steroids causes degrees of depression and anxiety. Add to this the worry of the break-up of two of her grown-up children's marriages, the enormous country house with a sometimes unreliable staff, a demanding husband, and many social events to look after; for me to then appear out of the blue and cause a controversy, it is no wonder that she was having a very stressful time. No doubt, her health eventually suffered due to all these circumstances combined.

Of course I realised that my birth parents reputation was at stake, particularly, as I found out later, that my strict natural father had always lectured ad nauseam, that children came after marriage, not before. My birth parents were both highly respected pillars of Leicestershire business and social society and regular churchgoers. It would not sit comfortably for them to acknowledge an illegitimate child from the 1930s. As far as I am aware, only two other people in the family were aware of the situation: my mother's sister, Gwen, and her husband, a surgeon who lived in Wolverhampton. They were both instrumental in guiding my mother through her difficult period of confinement and my subsequent birth. It is hard to imagine, in these days of liberal attitudes to children out of wedlock, how utterly different and difficult it was in the 1930s, when most women were either sectioned or sent to restricted hospitals in shame.

It seems my mother, who was born on 11 February 1914, did not have a happy childhood. Her mother died when she was quite young, leaving her husband, Neville Thompson, to bring up Marjorie and her three sisters. Neville Thompson subsequently remarried; but, sadly, Marjorie did not get on with her stepmother or her stepsister. My mother also missed an entire year of schooling because her father and stepmother were worried about her suspected weak heart. She then had to go to a Catholic convent school with her stepsister, who was of similar age, and found it impossible to catch up her lost year. Marjorie was consequently very unhappy at both home and school.

Gradually, this led to her spending more time away from home, and she went to live with her aunt and uncle in a cottage called Tempsford in Sutton Cheney, opposite the Hall farm where I visited in November 1981 as part of my initial search. I recall she was told by her stepmother that, as she was not regularly living at home, she would lose the use of her bedroom altogether, and so it was.

After leaving school, my mother went to work as a junior secretary for a large department store in Leicester, called Adderly's, and was paid ten shillings a week. Keen to improve herself, she spotted an advertisement for a secretary to a hosiery manufacturer in Stoke Golding and was accepted, following an interview.

During 1931, Marjorie Thompson, at the age of seventeen, became the secretary to Frank Hall, the chairman and managing director of Hall and Son, a thriving sock manufacturer in the village of Stoke Golding in Leicestershire. Marjorie cycled daily to work from the village of Osbaston, a journey of six miles. Frank Hall's son, Peter Hall, was due to follow his father into business once he left school. According to my mother's letter, when she first met Peter Hall, he was a 15-year-old schoolboy visiting the factory during school holidays. He immediately took a liking towards her. My mother said that she was not at all interested in him then, as she had already had boyfriends of her own age.

Peter Hall later joined the firm aged 16. After a few years, and despite the two-year age gap, he started to escort Marjorie whenever possible, and they gradually became good friends. Marjorie, possibly now living at Tempsford with her uncle and aunt, often divided her weekends between her three sisters, Beryl, Gwen, and Annette, rather than return to her father and stepmother; sometimes the insistent Peter accompanied her. Even so, she made sure of visiting her father on regular occasions, by cycling about four miles.

Bearing in mind Marjorie's previous unhappy background, it is not surprising that, over the years that followed, her relationship with Peter eventually developed into a full-blown love affair. According to my mother, Peter pursued her along country lanes by bicycle and on horseback across fields when the need arose. A typical bicycle journey he made was from Stoke Golding to Wolverhampton, a mere forty miles. He was obviously very smitten with this attractive and charming young woman. Unfortunately, this love affair resulted in Marjorie becoming pregnant with me in the autumn of 1935, when she had just turned 21, and Peter was 19. I was subsequently born out of wedlock on 3 July 1936, the result of a secret and passionate liaison.

I understand now that once Marjorie realised she was expecting a child and before it became obvious, she left her job with Hall and Son and went to live for several months with her sister Gwen and her surgeon husband, Jack Richmond, at 99 Tettenhall Road, Wolverhampton. They looked after her until her baby was due. This hid her pregnancy from family and friends, under the camouflage of problems with a previous, difficult knee operation. Imagine the upset this situation would have caused in those days. This was the house that Marjorie disclosed as her home address on my first birth certificate, although it could not be found during my exploration in Wolverhampton during November 1981.

Had it not been for Westminster social services unearthing for me the card with Marjorie's previous address at Sutton Cheney and my talk with the verger there, the addresses in Wolverhampton would not have led me to her in the village of Shenton, and I may not have found my natural mother at all.

I am sure that, at that time, Peter Hall did not dare risk going to his father, Frank Hall, to admit that he had caused Frank's secretary to become pregnant without any consideration of marrying her first. He may have been banished from his home in Stoke Golding and even from the family business. Who knows?

I assume my parents then had to make the very difficult decision to give me up to an adoption society. Imagine the trauma and heartbreak of the sacrifice of motherhood, followed by a living bereavement. My birth mother told me that she always searched the papers for news of me. I did not realise until quite recently, by rereading her letter dated 4 January 1983, that she had been given my new name sometime after giving me up for adoption. During the 1930s, adoption societies were allowed to tell the birth mother the name given to an adopted child.

I surmise that, following my birth and adoption, Marjorie returned to Stoke Golding in Leicestershire to resume her old job at Hall and Son, after an extended leave of absence for health reasons. I am uncertain of what happened to me at that point.

I presume that, after spending some unknown period in an orphanage or similar institution, possibly in London, I was adopted by Mr and Mrs Hughes and brought to Bromley, Kent.

Family records show that three years later, Peter and Marjorie Hall had a top hat and tails wedding in April 1939. Better late than never!

Marjorie's letter to me of 4 January 1983 still brings tears to my eyes. I am so saddened at the untold unhappiness she endured after parting with me at birth, all those years ago, followed by the stresses and strains in the family that she had for many years following my return.

She wrote:

> *I felt a different person after I had spoken to you on Monday evening, so you do see what effect you have on me, and when I type your name on the envelope, my heart nearly stops still, because I*

can recall when I got the letter from London (in the 1930s) to say that was to be your new adoptive name. And if there was ever a disaster of any kind, I always looked to see if your name was in any list. And I will admit I never thought I would ever see you again. Since we met on 20 October, I have wanted to write to you every day, but it's impossible with so much to do here. I cannot wait to see you again, and I still cannot believe it.

How clever of you to find me. It's such a wonderful story—in fact, sometimes I feel so proud to think you are my son, and I will really never believe it, that God was so good to me to give you back to me.

Yours with all my love,

Marjorie

Marjorie Thompson, back row second from left, Peter Hall, front row first left, on Cliftonville Pier mid 1930's

Peter Hall—RAF VR—1938

Marjorie Thompson—1938

Peter & Marjorie Hall's wedding—1939

– 9 –

MY NATURAL MOTHER
AND FATHER

Many years ago, but well after my natural father's death, I was given by my brother Neville a copy of father's written logbook detailing his wartime career in the Royal Air Force (RAF) and updated by him in 1980. It describes his reasons, at the age of 22 in 1938, for initially joining the RAF Volunteer Reserve at Leicester, together with his brother-in-law, as "an unconscious effort to get out of the rut". (Strange that I held the same views aged 18 and volunteered for national service, but in the Royal Artillery.) As a young man, Father was by all accounts a dashing young man, who was fond of driving anything with two or four wheels or riding a sturdy beast with four legs; he was also fond of pretty young ladies. At the time, he was just settling into the family business at Hall and Son, sock manufacturers. As mentioned in the last chapter, my natural parents married in April 1939. At the same time, I was in Kent and had just turned 3 years of age. Just five months later, in September 1939, World War II was declared.

Because he had joined the RAF Volunteer Reserve, the RAF formally called him up for active service shortly after the outbreak of war. He was trained on Spitfires, Hurricanes, and many other types of aircraft, initially as a flight sergeant. Thus equipped, he flew many sorties as a Fighter Pilot, escorting naval convoys over the North Sea and the Atlantic. Subsequently, he carried out weather and photographic reconnaissance after bombing raids. He was eventually shot down while flying an unarmed Mosquito over Holland in May 1943. After some weeks holed up at a farm, in a hut full of chickens, he was taken prisoner by the Germans. He was eventually imprisoned in Stalag Luft III, the infamous prisoner-of-war camp for airmen of all nationalities, until the end of the war in 1945. He was lucky to be alive. Had he been killed in action, as so many of his squadron and other RAF fighter pilots were, my mother might have remarried and moved to another part of the country, making it much more difficult or even impossible for me to find her.

I have devoted later chapters to expanding on Father's extraordinary escapades during World War II, based on his written logbook.

After Friday, 12 November when Marjorie Hall broke the startling news to me that her husband was my father, I was invited up to Shenton Hall on Wednesday, 24 November for two reasons. Marjorie wished to introduce me secretly to her daughter Carolynn, my real sister, for lunch in a restaurant near Rugby. In addition, she wished me to meet my father that evening back at Shenton. I was rather apprehensive. By now, I realised that he was very much opposed to my appearance a few months previously. However, Marjorie had told me that she would do her utmost to talk him round; in the meantime, I was to treat him as my stepfather at all times.

I duly arrived at Shenton late morning, and Marjorie drove me down in her Rover to the Dun Cow Hotel at Dunchurch, near Rugby. Carolynn was there to meet us; she was a most charming and attractive younger woman, with two boys at Bilton Grange, a local preparatory school. It was very exciting and great fun to meet her. She was the first member of the family that Marjorie had told about me, in strict confidence. Wow, I had a good-looking sister with style. The three of us chatted about our different lives.

I was delighted and relieved that they were so happy to embrace me, even if my father wasn't. I had agreed to Marjorie's idea that, if we should unexpectedly meet with any of her friends or acquaintances in the area, I would be introduced as a nephew on her side of the family. I did not mind that in the least and promised to be the epitome of discretion.

I finally met Peter Hall that evening at Shenton Hall when he arrived back from the factory at about six. Marjorie and I were in the morning room, and he just walked quietly in, and Marjorie introduced me to him. He was very charming and stimulating to talk to. We drank a glass of sherry, Croft Original—his favourite, I eventually learned—in front of an enormous log fire before dinner. We chatted in a friendly way about all types of subjects but steered clear of anything relating to my sudden appearance that summer. He asked me questions about my family and my career, particularly about events such as the Horse of the Year Show and other sporting events at the Wembley Stadium Complex. Marjorie left the room to ensure the cook had dinner well in hand, and we ate well a little later and talked more about life in the Midlands. I felt that, under the circumstances, I was made most welcome as a guest. Inevitably, I found it a little strange talking to my so-called stepfather, who felt perhaps too embarrassed to admit to being my father.

Over the years, I learnt a lot more about my father and the family hosiery manufacturing business, Hall and Son, which reached its centenary on 13 September 1982. I also learnt about his use of a small Cessna aircraft, parked in a hangar in a local field, to fly around the country to visit customers. Here was a man with the courteous manners of a typical country squire; he was confident but very formal, stern, and slightly intimidating. I gleaned much later that he had been a joint master of the local Atherstone Hunt some years before but was now the chairman.

My mother was a vice president of the Leicestershire Red Cross and worked tirelessly all her life, collecting and raising funds for that worthy cause. Their social life, as I was to find out later, included hunt balls, summer dances, and cocktail and garden parties in the grounds of their substantial country house for both local and national charities; they also hosted clay pigeon shooting and many other events. The upkeep of this massive house, stables, and grounds was, by itself, a huge commitment for both parents. My mother, in the local village, was affectionately known as Lady Hall. To me, this was not just another world; it was another planet. However, I was never invited to take part in any these events. *C'est la vie.* I was only too delighted to be invited to visit occasionally.

After I took Marjorie to the Waldorf on 12 November, which was only the third time we had met, our letters became more affectionate, and clearly a strong bond was growing between us. I became used to calling her Marjorie, but had difficulty in calling her "mother". In fact, her numerous letters to me were always signed "Marjorie".

In one of my letters to her, dated 26 November (I kept a draft of it in my file at home along with as much family paperwork as I could), I wrote *"I was very pleased to meet my stepfather and overjoyed and delighted to have a new mother, but in some ways, I react to you as I would to an elder sister. You hardly seem old enough to be my mother, particularly with your energy and all the things you get up to."*

For my next family assignment, Marjorie secretly arranged for me to meet my youngest brother, Timothy. Neither of us was to mention it to Father. When mother privately told Timothy about me finding her and her wonderful surprise, he exclaimed excitedly, "Bags I the film rights".

Timothy was attending a sales conference and exhibition on behalf of the family business at a hotel in the West End of London. Consequently, it was easy for me to drive in from Wembley that evening. We had a very friendly meeting, talking about family matters. We had a lot in common, as I had just been through divorce proceedings, and he was in the middle of them. We both had two children to consider. Timothy told me that his parents didn't always see eye-to-eye.

He told me a little about his job with Hall and Son. He was the sales and marketing director. He had worked in the family firm for many years, since leaving school in 1967, and had, like me, attended technical college for further education. He had specialised in hosiery manufacturing, as recommended by Father. He was about thirteen years my junior, very amusing, and witty. Later on, I realised that he was the family joker. I think he was quite amazed to see how similar in looks we were, even at that age. Later on, referring to the *Centenary Booklet of Halls History 1882-1982*, I could see that I looked even more like Neville, his older brother.

The booklet traces back the Hall and Son history to when John Hall, our great-grandfather, at the age of 28, built a small hosiery factory in Stoke Golding in 1882. He was, at the time, working as a foreman for a hosiery manufacturer in Hinckley, earning two pounds a week. The business was principally funded by an overdraft of £1,200 from the local bank. The business, initially established as Hall and Geary Company, thrived and became Hall and Company.

John Hall's son, Frank (my grandfather) went to evening classes at the Leicester Municipal Technical and Art School at the turn of the century, similar to what I did in the 1950s, only for me it was architecture, not hosiery. He joined the company to assist his father. Eventually, Frank was made a partner, and the firm was renamed Hall and Son and continued to expand. John Hall died in 1923, and his son took over. In 1932, Frank's son, Peter Hall, joined the firm after completing his studies, like his forebears before him.

Frank Hall sold the company to his son, Peter, in 1949. There followed another steady expansion, and eventually the next generation of sons, Neville, Michael, and Timothy joined the firm to assist their father. My three brothers and sister were all educated at public schools; the boys, like Father, at Wellingborough School, and Carolynn at St George's School for Girls, Ascot. Over the years, their company had manufactured socks for farmers, soldiers, and then the general public as well. During the sixties, the celebrities like Kenneth Horne, Lady Lewisham, Mai Zetterling, and the wrestlers Big Daddy and Big Jim assisted in marketing Halls socks. This was depicted in the centenary booklet. The Duchess of Gloucester and comedians including Derek Roy and Jimmy Edwards had also visited exhibitions and supported Hall and Son.

Is it any wonder that, with a family history like that, I felt the need to change my name back to the one I was originally given at birth, John Thompson or, as the eldest son of Peter Hall, I eventually chose John Thompson-Hall in recognition of both of my natural parents. Many years later, in December 2000, my brother Neville sent me a copy of the family omnibus tracing our family history back to the thirteenth century. I will refer to this later in the book.

Over the next six months, according to my diaries, Marjorie and I met twice more at the Waldorf for a tea dance, in December 1982 and then in February 1983; she was always dressed *beau ideal*. I continued to happily visit Shenton about once a month, bringing some of my music to play on the grand piano in the drawing room, encouraged by Marjorie. In one of her joyful letters, she said she was playing the piano one evening when Timothy arrived with his two lovely little daughters, and she continued to play while the three of them danced around the room. She said the girls obviously adored him and was worried how things would evolve, as he had just separated from his wife, Jane.

I can't remember exactly when it was, but about this time, Marjorie, escaped from Shenton and drove all the way down to the Onslow Arms at Clandon in Surrey, so that she could meet her new grandchildren for lunch. My son, Richard, then 15, and daughter, Kate, aged 14, had lived with me in the matrimonial home since my divorce in 1980. Marjorie was delighted to meet them and wanted to know all about their school and hobbies. I suspect they thought it a bit strange to now have three grandmothers. They learnt that she had nine other grandchildren to visit, and sometimes she invited them to stay at Shenton Hall. Marjorie asked my children if they would like to visit her soon, and of course they were both curious to do so.

My next important family occasion was when Marjorie arranged some tickets for the Horse and Hound Ball at the Grosvenor House Hotel on 3 March 1983. It was a very grand event, with hundreds of male members of the hunting fraternity dressed in scarlet coats and white ties, with their wives or partners in ballgowns, and the rest of us in black tie. Timothy drove our mother and his new girlfriend, Moe, down from Leicestershire, and I met them at the Hotel. The evening was an exciting event. The Great Room was laid out for a sumptuous banquet, lit by magnificent, sparkling chandeliers. We had a table for four, adjacent to a large, boisterous party hosted by Princess Anne. I listened, enthralled, to the hunting horn contest while we enjoyed a delicious gala dinner. Then we all joined in the melee of dancing, packed tightly like penguins on a crowded ice floe.

As the evening continued, Timothy's girlfriend, Moe, whom I had not met previously, remarked how alike Timothy and I were in our mannerisms for eating, talking, and so forth. This is quite strange, really, considering we were brought up in completely different surroundings and by different parents. I will always remember that kind comment; it gave me a great deal of confidence to continue to adapt to my lovely new family. I still had two brothers to meet and, perhaps, many more relations in the future. To demonstrate Marjorie's fears of being discovered at the ball with me, she said beforehand in her letter, "It's more of a large party of people than a dance; there are too many people to dance, really, and no one can really see you because it is all packed with happy, laughing people." She had to be very careful that Peter Hall did not find out. She must have been permanently treading on eggshells with him, experiencing a level of anxiety that continued for years.

Marjorie Hall, with left to right, Michael, Timothy,
Carolynn and Neville, between 2 and 9 years—1951

Brian Hughes at Bromley aged 15—1951

– 10 –

SPLITTING TIME BETWEEN FOUR PARENTS

In a nine-page, newsy, typed letter from Marjorie dated 4 January 1983, she wrote "I made a real effort and went to church at 9 o'clock," presumably across the road from Shenton Hall "to learn that the lovely rector from Bosworth is leaving us and going to Worcester Cathedral, and that I would like to go there for his installation on 12 March." The letter continued, "This depends on whether you and I are in Switzerland, but it would suit me to go after the hunting has finished, or would you rather go on the Orient Express in May, or shall we do both?" The typed letter continued to praise the hotels in Arosa and set out an exciting, detailed daily itinerary for the Orient Express to Venice and Rome. I have a photograph of Marjorie skiing in Switzerland when she was younger, and skiing has always been a passion of mine, ever since I was taught in the Royal Artillery in Germany on manoeuvres near Winterberg in 1955.

The year 1983 continued with a Mother's Day visit to see Mum at Hailsham in Sussex on 13 March, a two-day visit to Shenton to see Marjorie in the Midlands on 22 and 23 March, and then back down to Hailsham to help with my adoptive parents' large garden on 24 March. My own social life had taken off in Surrey, with regular evening events at the Wembley Stadium Complex and dinner dances locally in Surrey.

I made another visit to Shenton on 29 April. With the demands of my job and the children at home, I had, sadly, found it impossible to organise two weeks away on holiday with Marjorie at that time. I then received a handwritten letter from Marjorie dated 12 May. She wrote, *"Something has caused me to have an awful attack, and the pills for depression are killing me."* Sleepless nights followed. The letter goes on to say that her old trouble was back, causing the doctor to reintroduce steroids. After a series of tests, the doctors advised that all the pills that she had been taking for depression were wrong, causing her more harm than good. It took five doctors and nine weeks of tests to find out the best way forward. New drugs were introduced, including sleeping pills and tranquillisers, presumably to try and reverse the earlier side effects.

Sadly, by the end of May that year, Marjorie was admitted to hospital at Northampton with a serious, stress-related illness. It had resulted from her earlier temporal arteritis that began in 1981, before I met her. This meant that any holidays she had planned were put on hold. Marjorie's handwritten letter of 31 May 1983, from hospital, says:

My Dearest Brian, I am trying to get better, but my head is still very difficult with the 1981 problems. I am being treated for a breakdown. I blame the doctors. Peter has kindly visited me every day, and the family come regularly. P.S. This is only the second letter I have written here. The other was to my sister. My love to you, Marjorie.

I understand the usual symptoms of temporal arteritis vary with extremes of dizziness, deep anxiety, headaches, stiff neck and shoulders, high blood pressure, extreme tenderness of the scalp and temples, and feeling very grotty first thing. If symptoms are prolonged, people can feel awful all the time. Her previous GP treatments were a course of steroids which in themselves can cause depression. It was a sad time for me when I was asked by Father to stop visiting Shenton for some time until Marjorie was better. I felt so helpless. These difficulties arose again later.

Further letters from Marjorie in June and July said how difficult it was to cope with the new tablets; they were causing both eating and sleeping problems. By July, Marjorie was out of hospital and back at Shenton Hall. A very slow recovery began, which took many months. A nurse visited each day to look after her, and she went out occasionally, with assistance, to small, local events. However, she stated in her letters that she was not well enough to go on holiday anywhere at the moment. Fortunately, from August, we were able to start writing to each other again and also talking on the telephone occasionally. As I write this in April 2012, statistics published today by the National Health Service say, "Close on seven million prescriptions for anti-anxiety drugs were issued in 2011, a staggering number of people at the end of their tether. 17,000 out-patients appointments, four times that in 2007". An alarming statistic.

During March 1983, my adoptive father, Ernest Hughes, who was in his eightieth year, was admitted to hospital at Hailsham with a heart problem. He recovered after a few days. He was readmitted urgently on 10 May; sadly, this time did not recover from a second heart attack and died at 05.00 a.m. on 11 May. Mum was overwrought, as she was expecting him to return home, like he did the time before. She was not even able to be at his bedside just before he died. He was a regular smoker all his life, and probably overweight, and I suppose his heart and lungs just gave up.

As the only son, I was responsible for my widowed mother's welfare. I spent several days at Hailsham comforting Mum and organising Dad's cremation on 20 May. Phyllis, their best friend from Bromley, came to stay for a while. I managed to visit Marjorie in hospital near Northampton on 14 June, to find she was undergoing a thorough investigation into her medication and the reasons for her worsening illness. I took on the task of moving Mum, now in her eighties, from Hailsham back to Bromley, Kent, to be nearer friends from the past.

I found a suitable small house for her, carried out the all the financial and legal aspects of the purchase, and organised the subsequent move on 30 August back to Bromley and the sale of their bungalow at Hailsham. The new house was a first-floor maisonette in Bickley, a short bus ride away from Bromley and close to Phyllis. It was easy to look after and had a tiny garden. Mum did not have any experience with administrative matters, nor was she even familiar with writing cheques. Dad had always insisted, as the sole breadwinner, that he look after every financial aspect in their lives. Mum did not drive a car, so it was essential that she moved close to shops and public transport.

Thereafter, Mum spent many happy years at the Bickley maisonette. She hadn't been very happy at Hailsham, complaining that she had no friends and couldn't get to the shops without Dad driving her there. The move to Hailsham had been prompted by past happy holidays at Eastbourne. However, enjoyable holidays do not necessarily mean that one is going to be happy there full-time in later life. Nevertheless, they did enjoy outings in the car.

By the time Mum reached her late eighties, I had to move her again to Andorra Court, in a ground-floor, warden-assisted flat on the outskirts of Bromley. She stayed there for a couple of years before she said she didn't like being at the back of the block. Once a front-facing flat became available, I moved her again to the first floor, which gave her a view and the comfort of a main road to watch. With her dry sense of humour, she used to say she would live to annoy.

Unfortunately, some years later, she fell out of bed and broke her hip. After a lengthy hospital recovery, dementia occurred, and my daughter and I were asked by social services to find Mum a residential care home. We found a suitable home, at Chertsey, so she could be nearer to her grandchildren. Mum didn't like being there very much and didn't seem to mix with other residents. Although I had moved to Southampton by then, we all made regular visits. Mum eventually died aged 99 in 2002.

Returning to my story, the summer of 1983 proved to be very stressful, with Marjorie being unwell and Dad suffering his heart attack and dying. Later, my mother-in-law, who was also my godmother and to whom I was very close, became seriously ill and died on 26 August 1983. This was the second death of someone close inside three months, and it was a shock to me.

All through 1982 to 1985, I was driving from Surrey to Wembley and back for work. Every day was packed with managing the consultants and contractors, carrying out many projects and events on this thriving sporting and commercial complex. At the same time, as a single parent, I was keeping a watchful eye on my two teenage children. Fortunately, we always got on very well together, and their education continued without much trouble.

The next of my natural brothers to be told about me was Michael, and this happened in 1984. He was married to Eli, and they also had two children. Come to think about it, Carolynn and Timothy had two children; this was quite a theme for us all so far. Michael, three years older than Timothy, lived in Oslo, Norway, at that time but had previously worked in the family firm with Timothy and Neville after leaving school. After Michael's marriage to Eli, they lived in England, and Michael worked at Hall and Son and was responsible for marketing. However, after a while, Eli pined for her Norwegian way of life, with the beautiful scenery of fjords and lakes, and in 1976, they moved to Oslo, Eli's original city, for Michael to start his own business.

On 21 February 1987, I finally met Michael at Shenton, when he came over from Norway to visit our parents. Eli was not keen on coming over too often, as she didn't always get on with Father. I learnt that Michael also played the piano, and we had both been choir boys when we were younger, singing Ave Maria and other church music on special occasions. Timothy, Michael, and I went to the church in Market Bosworth that weekend, where Carolynn was arranging flowers for a wedding. For a bit of fun, Michael and I sang a duet at full volume during the morning rehearsal. Michael is the tallest of us all and is probably still the most athletic.

Carolynn was known as the Constance Spry of the Midlands, due to both her wonderful flower arrangements for weddings, including a Royal Wedding, and the range of classes she organised to teach those skills to other people in the area.

It was the late summer of 1985 before Marjorie decided to tell Neville about me. It was still a tricky time for her. My father, apparently, was still very reluctant to consider a public acceptance of me and, although I met him again a few times, I did not dare let on that I knew Carolynn and Timothy or that I knew he was my father. At that time, he was chairman and managing director, Neville was the production director, and Timothy was the marketing and sales director of Hall and Son.

Mother eventually suggested I should phone Neville in the late summer of 1985, in confidence, and arrange to meet him secretly. We couldn't meet immediately, but afterwards, Neville wrote me a nice letter on 20 February 1986, saying how pleased he was we had met the previous week, and he was sorry for not meeting sooner due to long working hours and bad weather since the previous autumn. He urged me to meet Michael and said he would ask him to phone me when he was next over from Norway.

Neville and I had met halfway up the MI, at a service station. He was the last to be told about me but was quite phlegmatic about it and welcomed me aboard. He was happily married to Kim, and they had three children. His letter of February 1986 states "Mother was a little better and was again making her own phone calls." This clearly indicated her illness had been more than troublesome. He added that he appreciated the delicacy of the situation between us all, shadowed by problems between Mother and Father, but he hoped they would realise that we should be able to all meet together, and then we could perhaps all relax about the matter.

It seems strange looking back now, thirty years later. However, such were the internal family pressures, exacerbated by our mother's ill health. It took from October 1982, my first visit to Shenton Hall, until the summer of 1985, for my brothers and my sister to be secretly told about me, one by one. Marjorie was thus in a permanent state of nervous anxiety for all of this time, hoping that Father would not find out she had arranged all of these forbidden introductions. This was accompanied by her intermittent euphoria resulting from meeting and phoning me and sending me letters, which I still have. These were sprinkled with phrases such as "lots of love", "don't forget I love you", "I think of you every day", and "hurry back here or I will forget what you look like." As if!

Many months later, I learnt that entirely at their own volition, Neville, Carolynn, and Timothy formed a deputation and asked for a meeting with Father in his office at the factory. They were extremely brave, as they knew Father's word was law both at home and in the factory. They told him with great courage that they had met me, one by one, over the years. They asked him whether it was not time that they could all, within the close family, accept me into the family as their brother and as his son.

I'm not sure what Father's reaction was; but I believe he agreed with them in the end, and thereafter this reduced some of the tension between my parents. However, I know it was still kept a secret from the wider family. I was still the obscure and unknown nephew from down south. Looking back all these years later, I feel sure part of Father's desire to keep me a secret was to protect the good name of Marjorie, his wife, to whom he had been married for forty-six years by the mid-1980s.

Of course, Father was very courteous and friendly towards me from the outset. However, my sincere thanks go out to my mother, sister, and two brothers for being very supportive and helping to smooth the path for me to be accepted into the family on a gradual and low-key basis. In particular, my heartfelt thanks are due to Marjorie, in the way she sacrificed a large portion of her energies and health just for me. It is that burden of her intermittent illnesses that I feel most acutely. She was a wonderful mother and grandmother to all her children and grandchildren, and this will be remembered for many years to come.

It is apparent to me, in hindsight, that my father, far from placing too much stern emphasis about the sanctity of marriage on his children as they grew up, was simply trying to protect them from repeating his earlier impetuosity of when he was 19 years old. The consequence undoubtedly caused much worry and upset to both my parents at the time and subsequently.

However, they did marry in April 1939, and in Father's memoirs dated September 1980, he said "Through the summer of 1939 all was bliss." I was by then 3 years old and living with my adoptive parents.

Mum and Dad Hughes with Brian aged 17—1953
(A rare special occasion)

Mum and Dad at Eastbourne late 1970's

Marjorie presenting a trophy to her husband Peter Hall,
for best mare at the Market Bosworth Show, July 1979

Peter & Marjorie on the lake at Shenton Hall—1984

– 11 –

HALL TOGETHER NOW—
A NEW SOCIAL LIFE

Marjorie was discharged from hospital in August 1983, and after a period of convalescence was well enough, by December, to visit London for a celebratory tea dance at the Waldorf.

After the deaths and health problems of family members throughout 1983, I took another visit to Shenton Hall on 29 December 1983, to celebrate a late Christmas. This indicated that Marjorie was a good deal better, and I visited again on 24 February 1984. After that, there is nothing in my diary for visits to Shenton until 29-30 December 1984, so Marjorie must have been unwell again for most of 1984. As a single man of 48, I had plenty of girlfriends, a varied social life, and a good deal of freedom by that time, despite a very busy period of responsibilities at the Wembley Stadium Complex.

The turning point was my next visit to Shenton for an overnight stay of three days, from 9 to 11 February 1985, Marjorie's birthday, and then again 23 and 24 March, followed by a visit to Selfridges Hotel in Oxford Street, London, for an evening dinner with Timothy, Moe, Marjorie, and me on 25 March, with further Shenton visits on 21-22 April. Marjorie was much better after nearly two dreadful years of misdiagnosis. She was at last getting back to normal, and the medication was better balanced and efficacious. Perhaps, by this time, Father had come to terms over my arrival, and there was less stress between my parents.

Around that time, Marjorie showed me a wicker shopping basket full to the brim with boxes of many different types of pills. Some had worked, and many others had not. There were a range of pills for the treatment of anxiety—a mixture of antidepressants, depressants, tranquiliser tablets, and sleeping pills. She said, "I feel as though I am being treated like a guinea pig by the Doctors. They are forever trying new drugs on me that have just come on stream." Father did his best by regularly ensuring that their GP kept trying to cure his wife, but one wonders why more notice was not being taken of the patient's abhorrence at this constant drug experimentation.

As a strange coincidence whilst writing this chapter, my newspaper front page headlines this morning, 2 May 2012, say "Lethal errors in two million prescriptions" and "Doctors are making mistakes in drugs given to one in five patients, with the elderly worst affected, says General Medical Council."

During this earlier difficult period, I asked Marjorie to leave the greyness of Shenton in the winter and come down to Surrey for a month's rest away from the worries of it all and let me look after her. She politely declined, saying, "Darling, I could not leave Peter on his own, or I might not have a home to come back too." This demonstrates how seriously affected she was by either the variety of drugs she was taking or her high levels of anxiety, or both. Part of her more natural aspect of treatment was to sit in front of an artificial light box for a specified period every day. Seasonal Affective Disorder, or SAD, is caused by lack of sunlight during the winter that can cause depression or, worse, inhibit overcoming existing depression. Light therapy works by resetting your biological clock timings (your circadian rhythms) to where they should be; that is, setting the body clock to July instead of December. Winter light varies but can be as low as 1,000 lux. Normal living room light is as low as 100 lux, but bright summer sunlight can measure as high as 20,000 lux. I can't be sure, but I hope that the light box did help Marjorie get better.

The national press, as I write in October 2012, reports, "It is estimated half a million people in the UK suffer from SAD." The newspaper report went on to say, the Metrological Office may soon be offering, by text message, impending gloomy weather reports, so that people can use these light boxes in an attempt to offset this mood disorder. Regular exercise and certain vitamins and herbal remedies will also help.

By this time, I was getting to know the Grade II* listed Jacobean-style country house very well, and it had taken on a homely feel at the ground-floor level, despite its vast size and volume. However, it was not a place to be on one's own at night time. There were too many half-open doors leading to dingy, poorly-lit cellars or dark, empty bedrooms and spooky attics, filled with aromas of old furniture and bric-a-brac. A few signs written in German could still be seen in the attics that had once been a prisoner-of-war billet. Creaking floor boards added to the impression of a past age, but it was fascinating nevertheless.

During the day, anyone with guile and cunning could have slipped through the back door, up the rear staircase, and hidden themselves. However, by early evening, all external doors were locked, and just before bedtime, the main entrance doors of solid oak were further secured by an internal heavy metal bar, slotted into the jambs on either side of the doorway. Father always set the alarms at night or, when absent, during the daytime. Then he fed Pepper, the long-haired silver Setter, his evening meal. Father also had sent rumours around the locality that he kept a loaded shotgun ready for any burglars and wouldn't hesitate to use it. Those were the days.

My brothers and sister must have had a ball playing hide-and-seek or other party games, when they were young, in such a warren of a house. Perhaps they were too scared. Some parts on the west side, at the ground and second floor levels, were left derelict and, apart from the external walls, areas of floor had rotted away. These parts were normally out of bounds, although I was allowed a tour which included the machicolated tower. This was the highest part of the house, with panoramic views across the beautiful countryside in all directions.

In the winter, it was not a warm house, in particular for ladies wearing smart clothes, as Marjorie did. The exceptions were the morning room, where invariably there was an enormous log fire with crackling flames, and the kitchen, with the oil-fired Esse oven on twenty-four hours a day. For men wearing thick, woollen Hall and Son socks, heavyweight sports jackets, and corduroy trousers, it was probably quite tolerable. The dimly lit but well-furnished bedrooms and bathrooms upstairs, despite their ancient hot-water radiators from a boiler in the basement, were not very warm either. However, aided by an electric blanket, twelve-inch-thick eiderdowns, and a generous nightcap, I slept like a log when I stayed there overnight.

Conversely, during a warm summer, the house was a haven of coolness, with its thick, protective walls that took all summer to become overheated. To keep her spirits up, whether busy or not, Marjorie carried a portable radio-cassette player around the house and garden with her. Two of her favourite artists were Richard Clayderman, playing a whole range of piano music, and Sacha Distel. She played the Sacha Distel songs over and over, to such an extent that Father often quipped with a dry smile "That Sacha Distel lives here." His signature tune, "The Good Life" and other hits, like "Raindrops Keep Falling on My Head" were a romantic tonic that helped keep Marjorie resolute under all the difficulties that I have alluded to in earlier chapters. I did the same thing during the latter years of my first marriage, in the car driving to work. The 1960s and 1970s were awash with a great range of music of all kinds.

Marjorie certainly had a passion for music and the arts, which many members of the family shared with her. I took up watercolour painting in later life. I also performed in two separate years in Gilbert and Sullivan's *Pirates of Penzance*, one of which was broadcast on BBC Southern TV. I was only a back row pirate and doubled up as a policeman, singing, "A policemen's lot is not a happy one, nappy one." Thereafter, over the years, I crammed in every classical and jazz concert, ballet, opera, and West End show and art gallery that I could afford the price and the time to go to.

The ground-floor morning room, separate dining room, and huge hall were filled with an eclectic mix of beautiful Georgian, Victorian, and Edwardian highly polished oak and mahogany tables and chairs, together with a continental carved oak bureau and buffet sideboards, filled with an array of bone china, glassware, and silverware fit for royalty, to my way of thinking. The drawing room was furnished with a Louis XV-style carved and gilt Duchesse, Louis Philippe-style giltwood salon chairs, a Victorian rosewood bureau bookcase, and a variety of other Georgian and Victorian items, making this perhaps the grandest of all the rooms.

The huge hall boasted a magnificent George IV oak grandfather clock, horse bronzes, silver cups from horse shows, oil paintings and water colours of fox hunting, racing, steeplechasing, and landscapes. Amongst them were some originals by Alfred Wheeler, Snaffles, James Charles, John Emms, Vincent Clare, and Heywood Hardy, nearly fifty paintings in all around the house. Deep, red-patterned Afghan rugs covered the stone flooring, and an elegant staircase, with paintings lining the wall, rose to a half landing on which sat a glass casing of stuffed birds of prey. The subdued lighting added to the mystery and ambience of this historical house. In unused parts, some of the carpets were slightly threadbare, accompanied by small areas of peeling wallpaper. The roof leaked in very bad wet weather, as most houses of nearly 400 years of age do, and it caused enormous worry to my parents, insofar as the plaster and woodwork was deteriorating.

As described already, the drawing room was by far the best preserved and grandest room, though hardly lived in whilst I visited. No doubt, in times gone by, it was the centre piece for many grand dinner parties and had its own magnificent floor-to-ceiling carved-stone fireplace, embellished with the Wollaston Coat of Arms. An eight-octave grand piano by the window was covered with family photos, including one of me requested by Marjorie. The floor was covered with luxurious, thick-pile carpets, and the furniture included elegant sofas. Although not warm in the winter unless the fireplace was lit, Marjorie placed a portable gas fire by the piano to keep the chill off. I practiced and sang to her, anything from West End musicals, Cole Porter, to Andrew Lloyd Webber. One particular favourite between us was, "All I Ask of You" from *The Phantom of the Opera*, which included the lyrics, "No more talk of darkness, forget these wide eyed fears; I'm here, nothing can harm you, my words will warm and calm you". The song had a beautiful melody and appropriate words that encapsulated the atmosphere perfectly.

Over the years, before I appeared, my birth parents spent many evenings entertaining in the drawing room. I'm told on one occasion during a drinks party, Father left the room and later returned wearing a wig and using a foreign accent. Nobody recognised him for ages, not even Marjorie. He just circulated as another guest!

In the main, we spent our time together in the morning room. Life centred on morning coffee or afternoon tea in the large bay window overlooking the stone terrace, with steps down to the herbaceous borders. These steps led to the manicured lawns and symmetrical rose beds, framed by the clipped topiary yew hedge, mounted by threatening peacocks. Beyond that were twenty-two acres of paddocks, where a few hunters peacefully grazed with their foals. Further afield, on the other side of the southern boundary, were acres of landscaped farmland, rolling into the background for miles, stretching to the village of Sutton Cheney, where my first tentative exploration began in 1981. To the left was a large orchard, and beyond that, there were huge clusters of mature, pink rhododendron bushes, with a woodland copse as a backdrop in vivid hues of green foliage in the summer, and later, glorious autumnal colours. This led, via a sweeping gravel drive, to the main entrance with majestic, pillared iron gates.

On the other side, over to the right and furthest away to the south-west boundary, was a very large lake, surrounded by pollarded lime trees. A stream from the adjacent famer's land fed the lake. It then gently flowed down a small waterfall under the overhanging willow trees, adjacent to the Antiques Centre in the village of Shenton. Sometimes during a very hard winter, the family ice-skated on the lake.

In the morning room bay window, Father had his favourite armchair to relax in with a newspaper or magazine and to smoke his pipe after an exhausting day's hunt or visit to the factory. Other members of the family were able to share this prized area through the haze of a delicious aroma of pipe tobacco. I revelled in this, as I had smoked a pipe in my twenties and thirties. Not all the ladies of the family approved of this pleasure, however.

On the table in the window were piles of magazines such as *Tatler*, *Horse and Hound*, *Motor Car*, and *House and Gardens*, reflecting my parents' interests and hobbies.

The tall, Victorian, oak bookcase was crammed with books about fox hunting, country pursuits, history, and geography; there were autobiographies, fiction paperbacks, and some very serious hardbacks. There were other bookcases in this room and around the house with books handed down the generations and collected over a lifetime. Opposite from the Victorian bookcase sat a Victorian, carved-oak twin pedestal desk with matching chair. By far the most stunning aspect of this room was the magnificent, carved-wood surround and overmantel, possibly of seventeenth-century Spanish origin, framing the huge, log-burning fireplace.

Probably the next most important room in the house by Father's reckoning, other than his bedroom, was the tack room. Originally an oak-panelled study, this room was tucked in behind the kitchen, and was in easy reach of the stables through the back door. Expensive leather hunting saddles were draped over a wrought-iron bench frame, and pairs of black-spurred hunting boots were cleaned and highly polished, together with leather harnesses and different types of bridles and head collars. Black bowlers and silk top hats sat on oak shelves. Rosettes festooned the walls, some quite old and faded; scarlet hunting coats, black hunting coats, and several off-white pairs of hunting breeches were suspended around the walls. This was an Aladdin's cave of equestrian paraphernalia, the air heavy with the aroma of mature leather. What had I missed over the years?

The treasures in the tack room reminded me of my early twenties, when I bought an off-white riding mackintosh with a red, felt inner lining for everyday use, and my friends would ask me, "Where's your horse?" I should have replied, "It's in my DNA," but I had no idea at the time about my real ancestry or what was ahead of me, as most of us rarely do.

Further along the rear corridor was a small, linenfold-panelled room, furnished as a study, with a secret door to a water closet. On the other side of the back corridor was a billiard room with a full-size billiard table at which I had the pleasure of playing snooker with Father on my occasional visits, but only in the summer. In the winter, it was too cold and damp in that room, as it was several steps down from the ground-floor level and was directly next to the ancient, derelict kitchen area. The adjacent corridor led through a deserted and derelict inner courtyard to a covered swimming pool.

The pool was about fifty feet by twenty feet, surrounded by pale-yellow Yorkstone paving. It was constructed as a previous extension between the west boundary of the house and the walled kitchen garden. The modern, curved steel roof beams that held up the heavy-duty polythene roof were supported on the remains of the original kitchen garden walls that ran around the pool and right up to the house. The roof was permanently held up by a heat exchanger unit that converted air to warm the pool water; this was filtered in the adjacent plant room, using excess cool air to pressurise the air space, backed up by a stand-by generator.

With solar gain, it was a hot retreat in the summer for swimming and a super-hot greenhouse for Father to grow masses of tomatoes and courgettes in raised beds around the perimeter. He also nurtured a prolific grapevine across an indoor trellis and over the roof of a small greenhouse. I enjoy gardening and often spent hours helping Father prune the plants and weed the borders, and I kept the area tidy and well-watered on my occasional visits. Marjorie made sure that I was able to go home with fruit and vegetables from the pool area and the kitchen garden, and she also gave me complimentary socks from her present cupboard; the boys used to secretly bring them back for her from the factory in Hinckley.

During bad winters, a heavy snowfall would push the polythene roof of the swimming pool down by overcoming the positive air pressure from the heat exchanger and put tremendous strain on the old walls. This required the snow to be immediately shovelled off at whatever time of day or night!

At the far west side of the house, at the first-floor level, were two small, self-contained flats. One was for the resident housekeeper and her husband and the other for the groom. Before I appeared, I understand it was possible to get a good housekeeper couple to live in through advertising in *The Lady* magazine and grooms from the *Horse and Hound*, for example. Local village people could provide a gardener and a cook for the evening and other part-time labour at peak times. But as time progressed, my parents found it difficult to keep staff in such an isolated village, miles from a city, although it was near the country town of Market Bosworth. Marjorie always made a point of working with the housekeeper, but after she became ill, help in the house started to become more difficult to obtain, and it was expensive to get people from further afield. Sometimes they didn't stay for very long, whether they were resident or visiting staff.

With my early construction and architectural training and experience refurbishing old buildings and churches, Shenton Hall was the large house I had always dreamed of, and ten times as large. I was able to explore the roof, the attics, and any room, and give advice on the damp and dry rot problems. I was in my element.

Outside was another tack room, a feed room for the horses, and a garage for the large horse box. This was used to transport horses for hunting and to carry animals to other fields to even out the grass consumption. There were two more garages for my parents' cars, four stores, a separate garden store, and a garden workshop full of amazing tools and machinery for a parkland estate.

Behind the stable block was a Grade II* listed dovecote, which can be seen from the road behind locked gates. It is reputed to be one of the very few working examples in the Midland counties or even further afield. Further along the road, by the wooden gates into the cobbled courtyard, stands a two-storey gatehouse which might have originally led horse-drawn carriages straight onto the gravel driveway in front of the house. This entrance has been closed for a considerable time, and the rooms above it were empty and unused. The main entrance doors are on the east elevation and can be accessed from double wrought-iron gates, with supporting brick and stone pillars, further eastwards on the road boundary.

In summary, the pedigree of this Jacobean-style country house, by any standards, was an exquisite example of rich history. It had a fascinating ambience, with a wealth of furniture, artefacts, paintings; a fine stable of hunters, mares, and foals; and extensive gardens, parkland, and a manage. Was it any wonder that Father was reluctant to leave it all in someone else's hands whilst he went on holiday? My parents had not been away on holiday together for many years. It was a huge responsibility for my parents to manage, and they must have worked extremely hard over several decades to restore and then maintain this exceptional house.

Shenton Hall—the Master Bedroom

Shenton Hall—the Drawing Room showing the Wollaston Coat of Arms

Shenton Hall—the Main staircase

Shenton Hall—the Morning Room

Aerial view of Shenton Hall

Marjorie Hall early 1970's

Brian Hughes at the piano, Drawing Room, Shenton Hall circa 1985—
the 'Nephew from the South'

Peter Hall with Hall & Son company aircraft a Helio H-395 Super Courier,
at the hangar, Shenton—1980's

Father's Retirement Party, from left to right, Neville, Father, Marjorie,
Carolynn, Timothy and Michael—1986

Brian Hughes age 32—1968

Brian Hughes aged 52—1988

Richard and Kate Hughes at Richard's wedding—1990's

Neville, Michael, Carolynn, Brian and Timothy in Neville's garden at the
Wedding of Georgina Hall and Charles Baker—2001.

Father in 1985 aged 69

Brian now renamed John, in 2012 aged 76

– 12 –

WHITE STALLIONS IN VIENNA

During the spring of 1985, it surprised me that Father agreed that he and Marjorie and I should take a short holiday in Vienna. Father was employing at that time John Price, a gardener and general handyman who was very trustworthy and lived in the village, and a lady groom called Geraldine, from Market Bosworth. She had worked with horses for a very long time. Marjorie was not entirely happy about her husband hiring female grooms; she said they were not as reliable as the men and could cause unrest if they were attractive.

I think the main attraction about Vienna for Father, who rarely went on holiday, was the opportunity, as suggested by me, to visit the elite Spanish Riding School to see the Lipizzaner Stallions. These originated in Lipizza in Yugoslavia in the sixteenth century, where they formed the Royal Court Stud in 1580. The Stallions, of Spanish origin, perform at the Baroque Imperial Riding Hall in Vienna. This was built in 1735, during the reign of Emperor Karl VI, and has been used for the training of horses for equitation and war since the 1890s.

Both parents needed a break from Shenton. Father was a passionate, outstanding horseman and horse breeder. Marjorie shared this passionate interest in horses. Consequently, both looked forward keenly to the visit. The horses in Vienna represented classical dressage and the Spanish Riding School was, at the time, the oldest and last riding school in the world which perfected riding in its purest form to international acclaim. The nearest we have to this in England is dressage at equestrian events.

Earlier in the 1980s, the Spanish Riding School put on a spectacular series of performances at the Wembley Arena, where I had the privilege to enjoy balcony seats for lunch in the directors' box. I looked forward to the trip and the opportunity to share my experience with my parents.

Via Austro Tours, I arranged for the three of us to stay overnight at the Grade II listed Grimsdyke Hotel, just a few miles north of the Wembley Stadium Complex. The Hotel as well as its forty-nine acres of gardens was purchased by W.S. Gilbert in 1890, famed for writing the lyrics in the Gilbert and Sullivan operettas. We flew from Heathrow Airport with Austrian Airlines the following day, 9 May 1985.

Our hotel in Vienna was the Romischer Kaiser, in the city centre. We spent an exciting time visiting the *Schloss Schonbrunn*, the imperial residence acquired by Emperor Maximilian II in 1569. It is a most beautiful and enormous palace, rebuilt by Franz Josef I in 1696 after it was destroyed by the Turks during the siege of Vienna. The magnificent state apartments had a breath-taking richness of furnishings and contained priceless, extraordinary works of art. The gardens would perhaps equal Versailles in France.

Austrians say Vienna is called "the Metropolis of Music". They regard this sobriquet proudly and with some justification. Many famous composers have originated from Vienna, and the love its citizens and visitors have for music and the arts in all forms is legendary. This love persists to the present day. During one of our evening strolls, we found ourselves in a tree-lined park called Platz Burggarten. In the distance, we heard the sound of music, and then we came across a small group of musicians and couples dancing on a terrace under the trees lit by twinkling lanterns. It was dark by then. We moved to a table for a digestif, and soon my father invited Marjorie to dance to a lovely waltz.

Victor Zuckerkandl, the Viennese musicologist, wrote that "with a waltz, something happens to music, and it's not that music does something to a waltz". Indeed, melodies in three-quarter time seem to acquire a life for themselves, never wanting to end.

It was a far call from all the stressful interludes that had occurred since my first visit to Shenton in 1982. I shall always remember, with pride, the happy time I shared with my natural parents in Vienna, one of the finest capital cities in Europe. None of us knew that time was ebbing away for experiences of this kind to occur. We visited St Stephen's Cathedral and, on the Saturday evening, went with tickets I had pre-booked for an evening Waltz and Operetta Konzert at the Weiner Hofburg, with music by Johann Strauss and Franz Lehar. During one afternoon, we ventured onto the wide and fast-flowing Danube for a fascinating boat trip.

En route on Sunday morning to watch the Lipizzaner Stallions, we stopped and stood at the main doors in the porch of St Stephen's Cathedral and listened to the wonderful singing of the Vienna Boys' Choir during mass. The cathedral was so full we could not even enter the building.

Still in the old part of the city, we found the Imperial Riding Hall. It has been renamed and is now called the Winter Riding Hall. We watched in awe at the brilliance of the Lipizzaner Stallions that, after years of training, had perfected 'airs above the ground', jumps known as the levade, capriole, and courbette. Father explained the finer points of this outstanding performance to me. The programme featured eight stallions, and all had extraordinary names; for example, Siglavy Europa ridden by First Chief Rider Lauscha and Favory Troja ridden by Chief Rider Tschautscher. They performed a series of steps and movements: pas de deux, short hand rein, on the long rein, and a school quadrille, all to music by various composers, such as Mozart, Boccherini, and Chopin.

We were only away from home for four nights, but Vienna was a very memorable trip for all of us.

Around that time, Marjorie wished to visit Devon to witness the start of a single-handed sailing voyage across the Atlantic by Simon Wall, the son of one of her close friends, whom she had helped with sponsorship for the voyage. So after a meeting in London on the Monday afternoon, I drove up to Shenton for a late supper. Early the following morning, with Father's permission and using Marjorie's Rover, I drove her down to Axmouth near Seaton, a popular seaside resort. Marjorie told me a few times to "Mind the kerb!" We were not far from Lyme Regis, where, as a young boy, I spent many happy times with my adoptive parents.

We had lunch with John Freeman, a very good friend of the Hall family, at Haven Cliff House, which overlooked the sea. He was well-known in Leicestershire for manufacturing caravans and motor boats. He had retired, with his new wife, to a lovely old property which was a much smaller edition of Shenton Hall, but it was nevertheless very attractive and comfortable and probably a lot warmer in the winter.

After lunch, I drove Marjorie and myself down to the sea at Seaton and along the coast to Beer, a mere two miles away, and showed her the beach where, as a very young boy, I went mackerel fishing with my adoptive father. Marjorie was delighted with the unplanned coincidence and thrilled that we could both be there together, some forty years later, as was I. We walked around the village, and it had hardly changed. There were still a small number of fishing boats drawn up on the tiny, pebbly beach, with rusty chains for pulling the boats ashore. It was blissfully peaceful after the mad rush of London.

We stayed the night at Haven Cliff, and the next day we drove to Plymouth. It was quite a long route, unaided by a modern satnav; I just trusted old-fashioned map reading. We arrived on time, parked the car by the waterfront, and met Simon, together with a large crowd of well-wishers of all ages. After Marjorie and I heard the refrains of "bon voyage", "best wishes", and "good luck" from all around us, Simon sailed slowly away out of the harbour, and we returned to the car and headed back to Axmouth to stay another night. On the third day, after breakfast, we bade our fond farewells to John and his wife and drove back to Shenton for an evening dinner.

I'm delighted to say that visits to Shenton resumed on a more regular basis, although Marjorie had still not entirely recovered from her earlier illnesses. One day, Marjorie, Peter, and I (still masquerading as Marjorie's nephew from the South) called into a local garden centre. We bumped into Sandy and Valerie Wollaston, the descendants of the original owners of Shenton Hall. The family had owned the house since it was built in 1629 until just before World War II, in the late 1930s.

I was introduced as Marjorie's nephew and, without a bat of an eyelid, Valerie exclaimed, "Oh, I can see you're a Hall!" We all smiled. I said nothing, but it seems my cover had been blown! I did, of course, look very similar to Neville and Tim, at various times of our lives.

When not managing the family business, Father's main interest was breeding hunters from two of his favourite mares, who were covered, when in season, at the Massarella Stud Farm near Bradgate Park, in Leicestershire. The foals were usually born in the spring, and Father spent the odd night in the stables with whichever groom he had at the time, checking the mare or assisting with the birth. Sometimes the vet had to be called in for difficult cases. The groom then nurtured the foal and, with its mother, it was entered at horse shows in various classes all over Leicestershire and the adjacent counties during the summer, with considerable success.

Geraldine, an attractive 40-year old divorcee had, over the years, become a regular figure in the yard, particularly during the hunting season. She was a member of the Atherstone Hunt, of which Father had been joint master and then later the chairman. Soon Geraldine became joint master and was responsible for checking the next locations for the hunt, obtaining the permission of farmers to cross their land, and supervising any repair work that was required after the hunt. She was also involved in the overall coordination of the Hunt. As a result, she and Father had a lot to talk about. I got on with Geraldine all right, but Marjorie was not happy at the amount of time she and Father spent chatting, out of earshot. On the other hand, I expect Father needed extra help with the transportation of horses and many other organisational matters of the Hunt, during the winter season when Marjorie had her illnesses.

Mrs Clarke, who gave Marjorie facials and health treatments, always warned her that husbands sometimes exchange their wife for a younger woman, and Marjorie should be on the lookout. I'm sure this was never Father's intention, but Marjorie, after years of cyclical depression and with her friends saying the same thing, must have been alarmed and despondent about the situation. It probably preyed on her mind; diplomatically, she did not discuss it with me. From other family members, I subsequently learnt that it led to one-sided rows between our parents.

In the summer season, Father won many cups and rosettes whilst showing mares and their foals. Although it is rather an expensive hobby, it brought both Marjorie and Father a great deal of pleasure and provided a break from fox hunting in the winter. However, it involved a lot of organisation, with paperwork, phone calls, picnics, and driving the horse box and

Range Rover from early morning to late at night. Much of this usually fell on Marjorie's shoulders, but she loved to be busy. There was little respite for Marjorie in the winter, with hunting on Tuesdays and Saturdays, with much the same amount for her to do as for the summer horse shows. It was a recipe for overwork and tiredness and would be for a woman even half her age.

I cannot remember attending many Horse Shows during the next few summers, as my parents were extremely well-known on these circuits, meeting friends and acquaintances at every venue. It would have caused further embarrassment for them both if my non de plume had failed again. But, during the winter, I occasionally followed the hunt with Marjorie in the Range Rover; not that we could see very much, despite the use of binoculars. However, Marjorie thought it important to keep an eye on Father to see which ladies he was talking to before, during, and after the proceedings.

I have to admit I became a little bored acting as a spy on my father. We were not able to see much of the hunting, as it took place mainly out of sight and well away from the roads we were on. It spread far and wide across miles of undulating fields and woods, separated by well-kept hedgerows. I would have liked to be with the action, but my skills at riding horseback were minimal and certainly nowhere near to riding to hounds. The entire close family were equestrian mad, attending all manner of gymkhana events, horse trials, eventing, show jumping, point-to-point, and county shows, probably as soon as they could walk.

I tried horse riding on holiday during my late twenties, but I didn't feel comfortable or confident in what I was doing. On holiday in Ireland, before the children were born, my ex-wife and I took a slow horse ride up through the beautiful mountains of Killarney, with a guide. I got separated from the main group, as my horse had a mind of its own and decided to turn off down a track to God knows where. I had no skill to turn it around without the risk of being unseated, and the stubborn mule kept walking. My wife at the time must have realised I was missing, so eventually she asked the guide to go back and look for me, whilst the rest of the party stopped to give the horses a rest.

The guide eventually found me, still seated and stuck under a pair of rotting timber trusses, inside a single-storey derelict barn; my horse was enjoying a rest and some fresh grass. I asked the guide in my best Irish accent, "Why did your nag bring me all the way down here?"

In his best Irish accent, he replied, "Well, sir, be Jasus, he used to live here!" The guide then led us slowly out, with my head bent low to miss the timbers, and we continued up the mountain pass. After reaching the summit and leaving the guides and horses behind, we all got into a longboat with four oarsmen for our next escapade. They rowed us across lakes and down rivers until we reached the point where we had started. "Where's the nearest pub?" was our immediate thought as we got into the car to dry off and recuperate. Nine months later, Richard was born. It must have been the Guinness and the mountain air!

Turning back to Shenton, to assist in my profile as the nephew from the South, which I didn't mind in the least, I decided I needed to dress the part. For warmth, I purchased a traditional Barbour coat from a local gun shop in Surrey. Marjorie matched this with a pair of size-eight green wellies, bought on a market stall in Market Bosworth, and I already had a sports coat and a pair of corduroys. So, with a tweed cap, Barbour, and wellies, I managed to merge into the mixed band of male hunt followers, some in tweed trilby hats. I was incognito. All the ladies wore headscarves, accompanied by the almost statutory green or navy-blue Puffa jackets.

In November 1985, as agreed in the divorce settlement, my children had reached the age where it was time to sell the matrimonial home in Surrey and share the proceeds with my first wife. Richard was by then 20, and Kate was 19 and working at Birds Eye frozen foods in Walton-on-Thames. I moved with them both into a very small, three-bedroom, mock Georgian terraced house nearby. Richard had just completed a two-year farming course at Merrist Wood Agricultural College near Guildford, and after describing the new house as a rabbit hutch by comparison to our previous one, he moved to a farm near Kingsclere, Berkshire, where he had a three-bedroom house all to himself. He started his farming career looking after a herd of 300 calves of varying ages; some were for the meat market and others for the milking herd. It was a committed job, seven days a week, to feed all that lot, and he did it for very low pay; but he had a scruffy mansion to live in. Perhaps the genes from his ancestry had finally broken through.

Both Richard and Kate had lovely double bedrooms at our previous home, and Richard was able to keep his entire complement of disc jockey equipment in style. When we moved to our new home, there was not enough space in the third bedroom, which only measured seven feet square, to store his equipment! I suspect he eventually sold it to purchase a larger motorbike, like his grandfather, Peter Hall owned.

At a visit to Shenton about a year later, Father took Richard down to his airfield a mile away to show him his latest aeroplane. Father was very impressed when Richard, after his training at Agricultural College, drove the tractor around to keep the runway clear of long grass. Over the years, according to my brother Timothy, Father had a Piper Tripacer, a Czech Aero 145, a Cessna, and then a Helio H-395 Super Courier for his various business trips around the United Kingdom. He also occasionally flew to the Channel Isles and France, just like the old days, but without the aggravation of being attacked by the German Luftwaffe. He navigated from landmark beacons on the ground after getting clearance from air traffic control in different parts of the country.

SPANISH RIDING SCHOOL
VIENNA

Morning training at the Winter Riding Hall 1890. After a painting by Julius v. Blaas

PERFORMANCES OF THE
CLASSICAL ART OF RIDING

Spanish Riding School programme—Vienna—1985

Neue Hofburg-Vienna—1985

The Great Gallery—Schloss Schonbrunn, Vienna—1985

Peter & Marjorie Hall dancing in Vienna—1985

– 13 –

ESCAPE TO SCOTLAND

From the lack of any entries in my diary for visiting Shenton during the winter of 1985/86, it appears that, sadly, Marjorie's cyclical illness had returned again. We resumed contact in the early spring, by both letter and phone, as she recovered slowly from the winter blues. I was invited to visit for the weekend of 6-7 April 1986, following my weeks skiing holiday in Austria. I found Marjorie in better health, and I visited again for another enjoyable weekend 17-18 May. I am delighted to say that by this time, Marjorie and Peter were making plans to take me to Scotland to inspect Father's forest plantations of commercial spruce, purchased in the 1970s and planted under a government tax-incentive scheme.

Investors were encouraged to plan for a long-term strategy to safeguard and enhance the environment, and for that consideration, the purchaser was granted tax-free income from future timber sales, 100 per cent relief from inheritance tax, and low exposure to capital gains tax.

I travelled up to Shenton on 26 May and bumped into my lovely sister, Carolynn, visiting Shenton for dinner, before setting off the following morning with my parents for Dunoon, west of Glasgow. We stayed at the comfortable Enmore Hotel, overlooking the Firth of Clyde, reached by a small car ferry from Gourock, on the mainland. We could see the Holy Loch base, one of the main naval submarine bases in the United Kingdom at that time, as we were ferried across the narrow estuary between Greenock and Dumbarton.

Father's investment amounted to a total woodland area of about 530 acres, with regular annual planting that started in 1972 and carried on till 1980. The woodland estate, called Trouston Forest, ran down to the water's edge of Loch Striven in Argyllshire. It had been planted with a mixture of Sitka spruce, Japanese larch, Scots pine, and other broadleaved species, and substantial growth had taken place since the seventies. It was stunning scenery. The main reason for the visit was to assess progress of this investment, but it also enabled my parents to take a break from Shenton. Trouston Forest was idyllic, even in the rain, at that time of the year.

As an aside, I believe that Peter and Marjorie had started to look at the possibility of selling Shenton Hall and downsizing in the area. They had visited a couple of properties in Leicestershire, but it was a tall order to find somewhere as attractive as Shenton, with all the same facilities, at the right price, and in the right area. Because of his busy life, Father had to go out at least one evening each week. This left Marjorie on her own more than she must have liked, and this likely played on her anxieties, particularly in the winter. No doubt Father began to realise the house had become too large for them to look after, now that they both had reached retirement age and in light of Marjorie's continuing health problems.

In Dunoon we spent many happy hours exploring, both by car and on foot, the beautiful forests and glens overlooking the blue, rippling stillness of the Loch; it was magnificent scenery. We met the local Ghillies out on the moors by accident, and then found a tiny village pub for a snack lunch. I had grown a beard by then, so I merged into the landscape quite easily.

Father's other reason for visiting Dunoon was to call in on his great friend, Digby Guy. He was the estates manager responsible for Trouston Forest. His wife was very ill with a serious heart problem. When Father returned to the hotel that evening, Marjorie asked him, "How was Digby's wife?" He broke down in tears when he said she probably didn't have long to live. This was an emotional side of my father I had never seen before, and he left the hotel lounge immediately to seek solace in their bedroom.

Father's other contact at Trouston Forest was a younger man called Winston Churchill, a mole catcher turned deer stalker, who obviously had humorous parents for giving him this name. Winston assisted the local Ghillies and continues to this day. My brother Tim still visits that part of Scotland with friends for various outdoor pursuits and calls on Winston for local knowledge of the wildlife. Our family sold Trouston Forest after Father died in 1995.

The next day, 30 May, we drove back towards Shenton, making a detour down the A66 to inspect Father's other woodland estate of about 60 acres near Brough in Cumbria. It wasn't as picturesque as Trouston in Scotland, but it was a similar investment. After a pub lunch, we continued our journey southwards. This was a very happy break from routine for all three of us. Father was most interesting and humorous to be with, and Marjorie was very happy at having me alongside during a holiday.

My next visit to Shenton was on the weekend 5-6 July, when unfortunately I experienced a medical problem inherited from my natural father, kidney stones. Timothy, or Tim as I now call him, drove me fast to the nearest local hospital, where they applied the necessary pain relief. The next enjoyable visit to Shenton was to see Tim and Moe, whom he had married, at the christening of their son, Sebastian, over the weekend 9-10 August at a small family gathering.

Marjorie wrote to me on 14 August from a hotel at Hunstanton, in Norfolk. My parents had decided to take a short summer break near the beach to visit friends in the area. Father also visited Bircham Newton, from where he did a considerable amount of operational flying with the RAF at the beginning of the Second World War. Marjorie wrote, "I saw how much better you looked on Monday morning (11 August) when you left, to what you looked like on Saturday (9 August), when you looked very ill and not my Brian! Do not work too hard—please delegate. Come back soon. All my love, Marjorie."

From left to right, Brian with Gillies Winston Churchill,
Tom Pearson and Father, Trouston Forest—1986

Brian in Trouston Forest—1986

– 14 –

NORFOLK, HERE I COME

In September 1986, it was Father's turn for some serious hospital treatment, so Marjorie whisked me across the country to Hunstanton, in Norfolk, on the east coast for four days, where once my parents had a small house close to the beach. I understand the house was swallowed up by the sea during the floods of 1953, caused by a North Sea tidal surge. I drove up to Shenton on 2 September, and Marjorie and I set off eastwards around the Leicester Ring Road and along the A47 in the direction of Peterborough. I had no idea what to expect en route, having only visited Aldeburgh, the famous music centre near Thorpeness, on the east coast.

Suddenly, we veered off left, signposted Stamford, and ended up parked in The George Hotel of Stamford, a lovely old coaching inn, which Marjorie and Peter had frequented in the past. Stamford is an architectural gem, a stone-built town of charm and grandeur. Walter Scott described the view of St Martin's Church, down the hill to the George, as the finest between London and York. We opted for a light lunch, and I admired the ambience of the place, which I would recommend to anyone.

We finally arrived at Hunstanton and alighted at Le Strange Arms Hotel, right on the coast, where Peter and Marjorie had stayed in August. I had brought with me a set of golf clubs. Although Marjorie didn't play golf, she walked part of the eighteen-hole golf course at Old Hunstanton with me. It was right on the edge of the coast, with the wind and sand blowing us along in the sunshine.

My brother Neville was staying at his holiday home nearby with his wife, Kim, and their three lovely, lively children, aged 9, 7, and 5 at the time. They joined us in the hotel for some meals, and Marjorie was in her element. She was thrilled to bits to have so many of her family around her, particularly her grandchildren who she adored. It was a lovely four days' rest in good family company.

It occurs to me as I write this chapter that perhaps Marjorie suggested that we went to the east coast, which my natural parents visited over the years many times since they were married, as a means of making up for the time I had not been there with her.

The year 1986 was very enjoyable for me. I had been a bachelor from the early 1980s and, particularly after meeting my new family, my lifestyle was much improved. I enjoyed various events at the Wembley Arena, including Barry Manilow in Concert, taking Mum from Bromley to the spectacular pantomime on ice, Whitney Houston in concert, and the Horse of the Year Show. Later, I saw Queen in concert at the Stadium with my lady friend and my son and daughter, various concerts at the Albert Hall and Festival Hall, and some West End shows; these were all very enjoyable and typical of a good year.

In between visiting Mum at Bromley and Marjorie at Shenton, I found time to play a little summer tennis and golf. I even got to an equestrian event at Hickstead on 25 August, with my divorced lady friend who had a charming house in Surrey, owned her own horse, and went riding every morning for pleasure. She drove me down through the country lanes of Sussex in an open-top car, music blaring, to meet her friend, Janet Brown, the female impersonator on TV. We all went together to watch the various events at Hickstead and to have supper afterwards in Janet's cottage nearby.

Later, my lady friend entered her horse at the Horse of the Year Show at Wembley Arena and won a prize. I watched from the reserved balcony seating, to the strains of the famous signature music, Mozart's 'Musical Joke, K522'. Wearing my security badge, I sometimes watched from the marshalling area backstage. The atmosphere was electrifying as I was surrounded by the leading top-class riders from the United Kingdom, like Harvey Smith and Nick Skelton, as well as their horses and many other international riders, waiting for the starting bell to ring. The smells of the sweating horses, saddle soap, and horse dung hung in the air and added to the excitement. You bet I was in my element! My boyhood horsey dreams, described in chapter 5, had been answered a thousand times over.

In the 1970s and early 1980s, both the Royal International Horse Show in the summer and the Horse of the Year Show in October were a sell-out. Eventually they moved from Wembley to Olympia or a Midlands venue. I suspect it was because a large proportion of the Wembley campus was occupied by hoards of caravans for riders and grooms, horse boxes, and practice rings for a very long time. Owners and grooms required this equipment as they prepared for, broke down, and cleared up after the event. This made it difficult to arrange alternative consecutive events on the Wembley Complex. It may finally have proved to be unprofitable compared with events such as pop concerts and ice pantomimes at the indoor Arena and football matches and pop concerts at the much larger stadium, all of which generally require larger car and coach parking facilities, and specific lead-in times. Notwithstanding the obligations of contractual agreements with the Football Association there was also the need to maximise the profitability of the complex as a whole.

The year was nicely rounded off with visits to Shenton for the weekend of the 15-16 November and 27-28 December. Both visits, I am sure, involved following the local Atherstone Hunt and formed a welcome rest from the rigours of my long daily commute (two to three hours) and a full-time job. It was particularly encouraging to find that Marjorie was in good health, despite the winter greyness, the enormous house, and her demanding schedule.

– 15 –

ESCAPE TO THE NEW FOREST

At the beginning of 1987, the Wembley Complex was sold by the British Electric Traction Conglomerate to a group of private investors. A new management structure was imposed, and it was a worrying time in terms of my job. Close members of the Hall family met at Kilsby, just off the A5, to celebrate Marjorie's birthday with a dinner on 11 February, and I stayed overnight at Neville's home, near Lutterworth. I went skiing again in Austria at the beginning of March with a group of friends including my wife-to-be, number two. On my return, I had a very cheery letter from Marjorie.

It was all about the lunches, dinner parties, and the Puppy Walkers Ball that she had been to with Father, Lady Dixie, and Tim's parents-in-law. She had lunch at Kings, in Hinckley, with her ladies club, followed by the Harborough Ride, a fundraising event for the Fernie Hunt, with sixty riders. Marjorie had injured her left leg in a muddy field and was forced to sit for several days at Shenton to recover. She said it was lovely to be waited on by Peter for a change. He had been obliged to get up early, turn off the alarm, let the dog out, and bring her a cup of tea in the morning. She said, "I must try and do the other leg when I'm better!"

On 21 March, I organised a twenty-first birthday bash for my daughter, Kate, at the Moat House, Shepperton, in Surrey, which included an early 50 year birthday party for me. Richard, now 22, arrived straight from his farm cottage, looking so immaculate in black tie and dinner jacket and a new crew cut that I didn't recognise him until he was a few feet away. What a credit both of my children were.

There was a visit to Shenton in April for a lunch with Marjorie and Peter in Sutton Cheney, where Marjorie used to live as a young woman. Marjorie seemed to enjoy revisiting her past with me, like the earlier visit to Hunstanton in Norfolk. There were more visits to Shenton in May and a long weekend in June when a garden fete was held in the grounds.

The Hall family event of the year was, without doubt, the wedding of my sister, Carolynn, to David on 5 September, in a marquee at her lovely house, Woolscott Manor, near Rugby. There were over 300 to the wedding and reception, followed by 150 for dinner. Unfortunately, Marjorie was unable to attend this wonderful celebration because of a recurrence of her illness.

My visits to see Mum in Bickley continued regularly; sometimes I helped keep her garden under control. I still managed to attend events at Wembley and visit a few West End shows in London.

January 1988 began with a family visit to Shenton and incorporated a celebration for the second birthday of Sebastian, Tim and Moe's son. I left the Wembley Stadium Complex during this month after thirteen years; the job had started with a two-year contract in 1974. Much had changed since then. Some of my business colleagues, who had previously been engaged on the Wembley Complex, asked me to join their consultancy companies, which specialised in the inspection and repair of road and bridge structures and North Sea oil platforms, as their sales and marketing director, and I agreed to the offer. It meant a lot of travelling all over the United Kingdom. This was quite different to my previous job, which had involved fitting in day-to-day construction work between sporting, business, and entertainment events on the Wembley Complex. My former position was full of pressures and demands, although I had enjoyed the opportunity, but I needed a new challenge.

I met my family again for dinner at the Hunt House, Kilsby, and was able to call in to Shenton in March and April when visiting clients in Birmingham. By June, I had moved down to West Malling, Kent, for a while to be close to one of the consultancy offices and was able to call in and see Mum in Bickley fairly regularly over the next few months. By this time, my recent second marriage had tragically broken down, and I was virtually homeless. Weekends at Shenton in June included another lovely day at the Ashby Show and again in July. Later that year, I moved to Bishops Stortford and rented a small, ground-floor flat in a lovely market town on the Hertfordshire-Essex borders, to be nearer to the other consultancy company. It was here that I joined the church choir, under the direction of Nigel Stark. Marjorie told me that during difficult personal times, there was nothing better than singing in a choir, and of course she was right. I made some very good friends in the process.

Many years later, after both Marjorie and Peter Hall had died, I found in Father's wartime memoirs that he also sought solace in a choir whilst a prisoner of war for two years at Stalag Luft III.

I had a very long and lovely break starting at Shenton on Monday, 12 September. We drove up to Scotland to visit Father's woodland estates, Trouston Forest, for a second time. It was even more beautiful in September than it had been in May 1986, for the previous visit. This was topped off by a restful weekend when we returned to Shenton. I was back again for a long weekend in October, for a lawn meet with the Atherstone Hunt, where I could witness first-hand the start and build-up of the day's hunting. Here, Geraldine, now called Geddie for short, was in her element and was indispensable as far as Father was concerned. Geddie's presence continued to be a huge worry in Marjorie's mind, but I could not intervene.

Marjorie's letter of 12 October said, "How lovely it was to see you at the weekend, but I find Peter so rude at times. I could really scream at him, but perhaps you did not notice some of the things he said. Don't forget I love you. See you soon. What about that, then? It's fun being in love with one's son. Marjorie." It was reciprocated in full, although I find it heartbreaking to read her letters, even after all this time.

After several months of serious confirmation classes, I was confirmed by the Bishop of St Albans on 27 November 1988. Marjorie and Peter drove all the way down from Shenton, which was an extremely kind act of dedication. They knew I was going through a very difficult and depressing time in my private life, yet again. I spent a few days with my sister and her new husband, David, in December before travelling to Shenton for a weekend on the 10-11 December.

On 12 December 1988, the partners of the consultancy companies I worked for, both good friends of mine, reluctantly terminated my employment due to the country's recession. They were finding it difficult to maintain turnover and staff. It was not a good time of the year to be let go; is there ever? Since leaving Wembley the previous year, I had travelled the length and breadth of the country with the two companies and clocked up thousands of miles, just like my father did before me. Only he did it in style, in the company's aeroplane!

Christmas came and went, but I didn't allow my redundancy to overshadow anything. As luck would have it, I scanned the adverts and saw "Project Manager required for prestige multi-million pound shopping development in Southampton". I went for an interview in London on 11 January 1989, and it seemed very promising. Just in case, I signed on the dole. However, I was called back for a second interview on 16 January and, after some discussion over terms, I was taken on. The recession went on for a further two to three years in the construction industry, so one had to take what work was available.

I kept my flat in Bishops Stortford, as the new company agreed to meet my hotel and travelling costs during the weekdays and provide me with a car. I attended my first site meeting on 24 January, before my official start date of 30 January. Southampton, here I come.

There are dozens of bed and breakfasts in the New Forest, and I chose to drive out of Southampton in a westerly direction and keep going until I found something I liked. Lyndhurst, six miles away from central Southampton, seemed ideal. It was quite a pleasant commute, after travelling all over England for my previous companies. I spotted a small hotel overlooking the Forest and booked a single room on a special long-term rate, as the hotel was undergoing refurbishment.

I travelled back to Bishop Stortford every weekend, stopping overnight halfway with a long-term friend. On the weekend of 29 January, my son, Richard, came all the way to Bishops Stortford on his motorbike to bid me farewell, as he was emigrating to Melbourne, Australia, to backpack with friends. His mother had relations there. I was very sad but tried not to show it. He had been a tower of strength to me since he was 12, and I had taught him all he could absorb as a growing teenager. We had our last meal together for a very long time in a Little Chef. He wore his black leathers, which, by the age of 24, he had grown impressively into.

Richard secured a very good job in Australia with an asphalt paving contractor. From his experience to date, he could drive any agricultural and construction vehicle with his eyes closed—even better than the Aussies! However, the Australian government refused to extend his twelve-month visa, despite legal representation by his employer, on the grounds that he was taking the job of an Australian. Sadly, he was forced to return to the United Kingdom only a year after leaving. He returned with a broad Aussie accent, having had a whale of a time sightseeing all up the eastern coast, scuba diving off the Barrier Reef, and visiting Ayers Rock in the centre of Australia. For half of that time, he was working on anything he could find, just to pay food and lodging, but he is a survivor. Around this time, Kate returned from a continental holiday with a street artist's portrait of her head and shoulders done in pencil; it still hangs in my study today.

Sadly, there was little in the way of letters from Marjorie that winter, but there was an improvement later on. In March 1989, I arranged a visit with Mum, now 86, to the Channel Tunnel Exhibition at Folkestone, Kent, which had been open to the public since 1987. We were both fascinated by the model railway exhibits that showed every aspect of the tunnelling work, the terminals, and the ancillary approaches. The display also illustrated the effect on both the English and French landscapes, at Ashford, the Shakespeare Cliff at Dover, and Sangatte in France. The project was monumental. A large mock-up of the tunnel-boring machine was built on the ground floor, and Mum was most impressed.

During my time with the consultancy companies the previous year, I arranged a meeting with Andrew MacDowell, one of the senior directors of the consortium of contractors, drawn from five of the most prestigious companies in the United Kingdom to construct the Channel Tunnel. I had met pipe-smoking Andrew when we both worked for Sir Robert McAlpine and Sons in the 1960s. At the meeting, we offered our consultancy specialist services for coatings to the Channel Tunnel steelwork, but so did thousands of others. We were not given an opportunity to tender.

April 1988 brought me a very interesting project to supervise and manage on behalf of my employer, Deacon and Jones. A very wealthy gentleman decided to convert an old flint barn to a luxurious, indoor swimming pool on his estate at Lambourn, Berkshire. After finding Shenton Hall, this was another jewel in the crown for me to explore. The final cost after a twelve-month contract was £1.2 million and a satisfied client. Did I enjoy the site visits once a fortnight? I absolutely did.

By the summer, Marjorie was back in form again, and I visited Shenton for the weekend on 27-28 May, 15-16 July, which included the Ashby Show again, and 11-12 August. I wrote to my parents, thanking them for all those lovely times and suggesting several dates that the three of us could visit my brother Tim and his wife, Moe, on the Isle of Man (where Tim had escaped to, fleeing from all his previous girlfriends in England). We took a direct flight from Birmingham to Castletown airport in early September, and we stayed at a nearby hotel for a week. Father persuaded the pilots to let him into the cockpit after take-off, and he spent the entire flight there, talking shop!

Father still regularly visited the new H.J. Hall Factory built in 1977 in Hinckley. It was much larger than the old factory in Stoke Golding. He had retired from the company in 1986 and transferred his shareholding in the company to Neville, Michael, Tim, and Carolynn. Neville and Tim became joint managing directors. In 1989, Neville bought Michael, Tim, and Carolynn out of the family business, hence making possible Tim's move to the Isle of Man.

It was a lovely break for us all, exploring the beaches and the Isle of Man motorcycle race route. This race is held on ordinary roads, with distances marked by lamp posts at regular intervals, some of which were rather damaged and bent. Tim and Moe lived in a lovely house at Ballabeg, not far from the airport at the south of the Island. Father made daily phone calls to Geddie at Shenton, to check on the house and the horses; unfortunately, this really upset Marjorie. My letter of 12 September 1989 said to my parents, "Thank you so much for the lovely holiday, both on the Isle of Man and our return to Shenton for the weekend. It has been ten days of peace and tranquillity."

By mid-December, with still another year and a half to go to completion of the Marlands Shopping Centre, I persuaded my employer to convert the subsistence and travelling costs between there and Bishop Stortford each week into a monthly subsistence to enable me to rent a house. This would show cost savings for them. I contacted a local estate agent, who sent me to two properties. One, south of Beaulieu, was small and an odd shape, and the other was a traditional four-bedroom cottage in the Forest. This was charming from the outside, even in the pouring rain, with one and a third acres of beautiful gardens.

It was a no-brainer to choose the second, and I signed up immediately after an internal inspection. It reminded me of a much smaller edition of Shenton Hall. It was only a hundred years old but apparently haunted. It had threadbare carpets, old-fashioned furniture, a 1940s kitchen, space for a log fire in the sitting room, and a barn large enough for three cars. It also included a stable suitable for just one horse—what a lucky break! I could make this a proper home, after the past eighteen months of renting several small properties in various parts of the country and moving from room to room in a bed and breakfast to keep ahead of the plumbers and decorators!

I wrote a letter to Marjorie dated 6 December 1989. Readers should kindly note the date, as it will soon become significant. It began, "My Dear Marjorie, I rang Peter this evening to find out how you are, and he told me you were in a nursing home at Nuneaton. I am very sorry to hear about this and trust you are being looked after properly and will soon make a full recovery and be able to return home. In the meantime, my thoughts are constantly with you, and I am sending all my love for a speedy recovery. Love from Brian xxx." Sadly, I never heard from or saw Marjorie again.

– 16 –

MARJORIE'S SUDDEN DEATH, 1989

I was holed up with friends over Christmas with a sudden nasty dose of food poisoning, when the police knocked on the door and said, "Your brother is trying to contact you urgently." I got back to Bishops Stortford as quickly as possible and found a telephone message from Tim and one from Neville, saying that Mother had died on Boxing Day. I was completely devastated, grief-stricken, and numbed to the core at this sudden loss to me and to the entire family.

No one told me she was ill enough to die. I would not have spent Christmas in the south of England, had I known. The funeral was arranged for 4 January. Father suggested I stay the night before at Shenton. I could not bring myself to do this and instead stayed with my brother Neville, at Lutterworth. Father rang me on the Saturday, and we spoke for over an hour about Marjorie, her illnesses, the funeral at 11.00 a.m., and the reception afterwards. I said I could not face going to the reception in Shenton Hall.

It was arranged by the family that I would follow in my car behind Neville's in-laws, Derek and Ann, who would escort me into the parish church of St Peter's, in Market Bosworth. As our cars approached the outskirts of Market Bosworth, it got tougher to keep driving. I was flooded with memories of all the lovely walks Marjorie and I had shared around the lake in Bosworth Park, joined by the fresh wind on a winter's day or the cool breeze of a summer evening as we said our goodbyes; these outings were, for her, a snatched half an hour from the constant treadmill of Shenton Hall. I've had to stop typing, as I can't see through the tears these memories bring, even twenty-two years later.

It was the car park by the lake that was the first place in Leicestershire that we met, during October 1982, just a little more than seven years before.

We arrived early, at 10.35, and the three of us walked slowly and solemnly to the empty church and sat in the rear pews to wait. Marjorie's coffin was already in the chancel. I shuddered—I would never see her again. The last holiday that I got to spend a lot of time with my parents was on the Isle of Man, the previous September. It wasn't unusual for me not to see Marjorie during the winters some years, and I had been asked by Father to stay away until she got better on more than one occasion, so I had lived in hope that she would recover every spring.

The elderly organist played nervously—hitting some wrong notes—and looked hesitantly down the knave as some mourners gathered slowly in the pews in front of us to pay their last respects. The clergy scurried in and out of the vestry with grave faces. I sat and said very little to Derek. The trauma of the occasion was overwhelming. Where were the rest of my family, all twenty-five of them? The minutes ticked by interminably. Was eleven o'clock ever going to come? Had Father broken down uncontrollably? I knew not. Suddenly, at precisely three minutes past eleven o'clock, with the church overflowing except for the reserved family seats, the clergy sped to the back of the church, their rubber shoes squeaking on the polished-stone floor. All around me were people I did not know, and not many were in dark clothes. How could they?

The main doors reopened, and although none of us turned round, I could sense the clergy were leading in the family—my family. They came slowly, with heads bowed, and gradually occupied the front four rows of pews on the right-hand side of the church. The opening sentences were given by Canon Seymour, followed by the first hymn, "The King of Love My Shepherd Is". I knew it well, but it brought a lump to my throat. I couldn't get the words through my lips, for fear of choking and weeping aloud.

I stayed silent, reading each verse to myself. The words swirled around in my head, and my eyes were fixed on the coffin. Could my dear mother really be in there, just seven years after our first meeting? The Bible reading was followed by Canon Seymour's address, "To this loving mother and wife of Peter Hall, devoted to her children, Neville, Michael, Carolynn, and Timothy who will miss her sadly."

I wanted to stand up and shout, "I will miss her too. I am the eldest son—am I not to be included in those words?" But, of course, I didn't. Neither did I walk to the coffin and stand there protectively. I kept silent to protect the good name of both my parents, but it was extremely hard to do so.

"She was not only a devoted mother and grandmother," continued Canon Seymour, "but a friend to all those in need, in the church, in the villages, and at the Red Cross. Blighted by illness, she struggled on, putting herself last".

Little did those in the church know about the many additional struggles that Marjorie had to cope with over the years and overcome to stay alive, only some of which I have I alluded to in this book, in the interest of privacy for the family. They were all issues that eventually wore her down and reduced the strength of her body and soul to fight anymore.

The second hymn, "Lead Kindly Light" was slow and poignant. The words were exceptionally appropriate for Marjorie, and I was able to sing them. Here is the last verse.

So long thy power hath blessed me; sure it still

Will lead me on,

O'er moor and fen, o'er crag and torrent, till

The night is gone.

And with the morn those angel faces smile,

Which I have loved long since, and lost a while.

After prayers, the last hymn was also very well-chosen, "Now the Day is Over". I managed to sing all the verses until the sturdy and faithful pall-bearers appeared and walked slowly up the aisle. As they picked up the coffin, I was stunned into silence. They slowly filed out of the church, with all my family behind them and no one glancing in my direction. The remaining mourners left in twos and threes, followed at the end by the three of us. It was a typical cold and grey January day as we emerged from the stillness of the church, and I felt empty. Derek and Ann kindly walked with me back to my car, and I drove slowly behind them towards the village of Shenton for the committal in the smaller St John's Church, opposite Shenton Hall, with ever-lessening control over my emotions.

Napoleon Bonaparte once said, "My anguish at our parting runs through my veins as swiftly as the waters flow down the Rhone, my emotion thunders in my ears like a volcano." My experience at my mother's funeral seemed to echo these thoughts.

The nearer I got to the church at Shenton, my mind became made up that I would not be able to go into Shenton Hall or even the churchyard. I was speechless with grief, and I was heartbroken and angry at the way Marjorie had had to live her life over the past seven years that I had known her. I started to compose a few words to scribble a note to Derek, to let the family know that I could not go any farther. I slowed the car to a stop behind his and started to write—the tears welled up, and I handed the note—I could not speak. He nodded and said he quite understood, and instead of going to the churchyard, he just stood there protectively by my car. I was weeping uncontrollably by now. Enough was enough. This dearest lady, my natural mother, who meant so much to me and had given up so much for me, was gone forever.

The minutes went by, when suddenly my sister, Carolynn, appeared and opened my car door, and through her tears she pleaded for me to stay. "No, no," I said. "I can't meet people. I just want to disappear." She urged me not to drive away until she returned from seeing Father in the house. The minutes went by, and then Carolynn reappeared, still crying. This time she pleaded with me just to visit the churchyard with her, which I did—both of us supporting one another. Across the road and up the steps we tramped, slowly, with aching hearts and in floods of tears until we reached the open grave. The coffin had been lowered to its final resting place. The churchyard was, thank God, deserted.

We talked through our tears and held hands like young children. Carolynn told me of the last two hours she had spent praying with Mother, a week before she died, with two other church people who were elderly and respected friends of Mother's.

Those two hours were spent in helping Mother talk about her life, her regrets, her problems, and her guilt. Carolynn said Mother told these two friends of hers all about her first son, the trauma and extreme sadness of losing him when a baby, and his return in later life—and the joy and the difficulties this had brought. She talked of her life with Peter—her problems, her happiness—it all poured out, and everyone prayed. Several days later, according to Carolynn, other members of the family noticed how relaxed and peaceful Mother had become, different from her earlier, restless, tortured, and impatient self. They all thought she was well on the road to recovery, as had happened in previous years; but, alas, she died suddenly from a ruptured aortic aneurysm on Boxing Day afternoon.

We each plucked a rose from the flower wreaths lying on the grass and dropped them, one after the other, with a parting kiss and a prayer for eternal peace and solitude for our dear mother. I led Carolynn into St John's Church, where our parents used to regularly attend the Sunday service. This was really where a new chapter of my life started with such excitement and pleasure all those years ago, and now a chapter of it closes with such sadness.

"Please come and see Father," Carolynn begged. "He wants to see you."

"I can't," I said. "I cannot trust my emotions, and I will be of no help to him at his saddest of times."

"Just come to the oak room," she continued to say. "Just tell him hello in private and say you will ring him in a few days. Please come. I must go to him now—he is waiting." I couldn't thank her enough for her selfless and unstinting sisterly love to me that day.

I walked slowly back to my car, the tides of emotion and anger subsiding after what Carolynn had told me about Mother's last few days. Derek, bless him, was still standing by my car. He was my rock of the day, my Samaritan—such a kind and lovely man—who was head of a very large family, with lots of happy grandchildren. "Come on," he said, "let's go in, up the main drive." And so, rather reluctantly at first, I walked with him along the gravel drive up to the main double doors. I met my brother, Michael, over from Norway and gradually eased my way into the entrance hall, where Father greeted me. He shepherded me into the fringe of the close family and the guests. Thankfully, they carried on talking as if I was just another guest or member of this extra-large family.

After some time had passed, an unknown, middle-aged, well-dressed lady approached and introduced herself as Shirley. I could not readily place her in the family tree, from Marjorie's many stories of who's who. She asked me who I was, and before I could answer, she offered, "You must be a Hall."

"Yes," I said proudly. "I am one of the brothers." The dear lady seemed so taken aback, and she didn't pursue her line of questioning, either out of politeness or a wish not to expose her lack of knowledge of the Hall family. I was fed up with being the nephew from the South! We chatted on about other, more worldly things until I was finally rescued by Michael's charming wife, Eli, whom I had not met before. Did all my brothers marry charming and attractive ladies? It certainly seemed so.

I asked Eli who the lady was, and she replied that it was Auntie Shirley, the wife of Peter Hall's brother, Bernard. Whoops! Eli kindly took me around and introduced me to all manner of aunts and uncles and cousins who were equally as charming and friendly. Father had asked Geddie to be at the reception to help out where she could with the members of the family and their guests.

The reader may wonder how I have managed to remember so much detail of that day. When I returned home the next morning after staying with Carolynn at Rugby that night, I wrote an aide-memoire with the express purpose of writing about my unusual story one day. Strangely, my brother Michael did exactly the same thing about seven years later, following the apportionment on my parents' estate, after Father's death. Like me, he did it to clear his mind of controversial thoughts, although we had never discussed this similar approach beforehand.

Before Marjorie's funeral, I received a lovely calligraphy card from a member of the St Michael's Church choir, with which I had been singing in Bishops Stortford for about a year.

Dear Brian,

To comfort you in the loss of your so newly found mother, may these words help to ease the pain of your loss. I will think of you on Thursday, together with your father and family.

With Love,

Sue

Lord, make it not so,
That we in grief should keep
The memory of that hour,
When she found sleep,
And with it found your peace.
Make it not so,
That we should banish laughter
On the day when she once more
Is learning to be gay.
Make it not so,
That all our joy should go
When she whose loss we grieve
Would say, and by your mercy,
Even now does pray,
"Lord, make it not so."

Amen

Once I was back at Bishops Stortford, Sue and I met in St Michael's Church to say a prayer together for my dear mother, Marjorie. An interesting footnote is that the three churches I visited that weekend were all associated with Hall family names: Marjorie's funeral was at St Peter's after my father's name, the committal was at St John's, my birth name, and I prayed at St Michael's, one of my brother's names.

– 17 –

FATHER'S NEW LIFE

There is little doubt that when one marriage partner dies, the other is usually left lonely and bereft, regardless of how happy or unhappy the relationship was. Some marriages are a mixture of both, in varying degrees. David, my brother-in-law, offered some very wise advice shortly after my mother's death: in a situation such as bereavement, do not make any major decisions for the first two years. Whether or not this advice reached Father's ears, I could not say, but he certainly did not appear keen to move house. During one of our many conversations after Marjorie's funeral, Father said I could be more open about being his eldest son. It had occurred to me earlier that during Marjorie's lifetime, he was protecting her reputation by stipulating I was his nephew.

Father's activities hunting, breeding hunters, and entering horse shows carried on without mother, much as they did before, but with Geddie filling in to help Father where she could. It was, I suppose, the natural development of the friendship that existed during the last few years of Marjorie's life.

This did not suit all my siblings and their wives. However, some felt that Father needed companionship, not only to counteract the loss of a loving wife, but also to help run and maintain Shenton Hall, the colossus of a house which had taken a toll on Marjorie's health. As a recent outsider, I could see both sides. Father had known Geddie's parents since she was a child. He was still very much in contact with Geddie's father locally. It was not as if she was some stranger; in fact, it was quite the opposite.

I called into Shenton on Sunday, 4 February 1990 to see Father after a business trip and dinner in Bolton the previous night. Even after his recent loss, he was in reasonably good form.

The year of 1990 was perhaps ordinary by comparison with the previous years of my happiness enjoying Marjorie's company and then the shock and heartbreak of losing her in December 1989. I felt a huge gap in my life without Marjorie and could not bring myself to visit Shenton voluntarily. The prospect of visiting her grave at St John's Church in Shenton filled me with torment beyond my ability to control. It was eighteen months after the funeral, before my new partner at the time persuaded me to visit Marjorie's grave with flowers. Even then, I could not hold back the tears. But gradually, over the years, the loss slowly eased until the writing of this book, which has acutely brought back the sadness of everything that occurred in the latter part of 1989 and early in 1990.

In April of that year, I was invited to Carolynn's for the weekend, which included an exciting point to point, followed by a weekend at Shenton at the end of May. The events are just a blur until I made a series of visits just after Christmas to my sister's at Rugby to see the family, including my brother Tim and Father and Geddie. On 28 December 1990, I had supper out with Father at a pub called the Three Horseshoes in Stoke Golding, a village a few minutes from Shenton. Father was very fond of this pub, as the food was very inexpensive.

We were able to catch up on our news. He was coping with Shenton Hall with the help of Geddie, and I had spent an enjoyable year in the New Forest cottage with a special friend. The following day, I headed over to Lutterworth to follow the Fernie Hunt that my brother Neville had hunted with for many years.

In April 1992 I received a two-page, chatty letter from Father, saying "A group of thirty visitors have just tramped around the house, but left a donation for the Red Cross." Both Mother and Father had always generously supported the Red Cross, as Father felt the charity had contributed hugely to his survival as a prisoner of war in Germany. He went on to record, "Geddie had been wearing herself out playing hockey and team chasing and was now in bed with acute tonsillitis." He had come off Cyprostat and could now run up stairs two at a time (he was 76 at the time). He was pleased with my partner's suggestions to take special herbal tablets and was feeling a lot better and regaining a little weight now that his indigestion had improved. Plans were advancing for the garden fete to be held shortly at Shenton. He was toying with the idea of selling Shenton before he got too fragile to look after it but admitted it was a slow and difficult task.

I carried on normal family communications by letter and telephone with occasional visits to Shenton over the next two years. Father's letter to me 9 October 1994 is particularly poignant and says, "I don't really want to move from Shenton, but I have a smaller place in mind if somebody should come along with a good offer. My health goes up and down, and I have three strengths of pain killers to use, including morphine. The only trouble is they cause constipation, and getting the balance right for normal functioning is nigh on impossible, so I have to plan my journeys carefully."

The letter continues, "I am still taking all the different herbal products you recommended, and I do honestly think they have prolonged my life. I went cubbing last Tuesday for three hours with no ill effects. My PSA reading has gone up to 22, which is better than when it was 280! But I would like to get it down to 4 again. I have a bone scan booked for next Tuesday and was supposed to be visiting the Royal Marsden on 20 October but shall cancel that because I have a new lady doctor who is a cancer expert, and she has booked me in for a week's radiotherapy at Leicester during that week. It is intended to reduce the pain and stop it spreading too far into the bones."

"All this is making life tough for Geddie. She is doing a wonderful job looking after me, and trying to get in hunting as well. We shall have to get rid of some horses. She sends her love." Father continued by saying, "David and Carolynn, just back from Cyprus, took us out for a nice meal the other evening. Neville is in Austria on business. I hope he enjoys it as much as Marjorie, you, and I did so many years ago."

Sincerely

Father

– 18 –

MY NEW LIFE

On 16 January 1990, while eating my delicious egg and bacon at a bed and breakfast early one morning, I looked out of the hotel window, to where I thought I had parked my car the night before. It wasn't there; this was funny, I was sure it should have been this end of the car park. So, after breakfast, I strolled outside to look at the other end of the car park. It wasn't there either. I thought, *oh bugger, it's been stolen, with my winter coat and other clothes in the boot.* I called the police and my site office with the good news and was told rather cheerily by the local police that the car would probably have been stolen to commit a crime and by now would have been torched in the Forest somewhere, to remove any evidence. How comforting. "But don't worry, sir, we'll keep an eye out for it, and if anything turns up, we'll let you know," the constable said. I soon hired a car, but a week went by and nothing positive came from the police, despite my phone calls. After a few more days, I did get a call from the police.

"A neighbour in the road behind your hotel, sir, has told us there has been a strange car, like yours, parked in their road for nigh on ten days. Would you like to come to the station and identify it?" The police assumed it had been used the night it was stolen for a night-time robbery at the local mini store, to steal cigarettes, other goods, and the safe. The safe was dumped on the back seat and had collapsed it. Other than that, a broken passenger door and lock, and a few bruises, the car was fine. And my clothes locked in the boot hadn't been touched.

The following week at Bishops Stortford, I packed up all my belongings and, with a removals firm, moved lock, stock, and barrel, including my upright piano, to a cottage in the New Forest to start a new life in a rural setting. On 7 February, it was squally and poured with rain all day, but it didn't matter. I was out of my soulless, ground-floor, one-bedroom flat in suburbia and into what could be best described as a cross between a nineteenth-century vicarage and a gatekeeper's cottage on the edge of the New Forest, up a gravel track off the country road.

With the cottage's sitting room, dining room, breakfast room, large hall with a grandfather clock, ancient kitchen, four bedrooms, and a bathroom, I could at last invite friends and family for weekends again. The garden promised to be the largest I had ever looked after. It extended to well over an acre of grass, with masses of shrubs, a rose garden, an orchard of apple and pear trees, a vegetable patch, and a small copse. It was surrounded by thick hedging and perimeter trees for perfect privacy. If only Marjorie could have visited me here, she would have been thrilled to bits.

I had left behind my friends in the choir and a life very close to their church. I kept in regular phone contact with my adoptive mum in Kent and my natural father in Leicestershire. This went on for some years, interspersed with journeys north to the Midlands and even more years travelling south-east to Kent. Mum, at 87, now needed a lot of attention. I was the only family member who could help, and I continued to do so until she died in 2002, aged 99. She was a contrast with my natural mother in many ways.

After a few weeks, I had settled into my quaint old cottage with a mixture of the landlord's furniture and my own pieces that were left from two broken marriages.

Towards the end of 1990, Mum was brought down from Kent by a friend for a long weekend, and we visited many local beauty spots in this lovely holiday area. I had a job to get her to go back! The year passed by very quickly, with two construction-in-progress projects for me to supervise, a good fifty miles apart.

In the spring of 1991, part of the cottage and the stable block had subsided, due to the clay foundations. Contractors started with partial demolition, and then swamped the driveway with miniature piling rigs and months of rebuild, noise, and dust, which of course I'm used to, having worked on building sites all my life. But I obtained a substantial reduction in the rental for the inconvenience. March brought another Hunt Ball at the

Grosvenor House Hotel in London. I stayed at the Farmers Club this time, with my dancing partner, a blind date who was a girlfriend of my sister, from Warwickshire.

In April 1991, I had notice from my employer that my contract for managing the multimillion-pound shopping centre would end on 31 May, as the construction had been completed. Due to the continuing recession, they had no further work for me. At the ripe old age of 55, this was the second redundancy I experienced in two and a half years. I had already had enquiries from a lady business owner in Southampton for house-sharing possibilities, so we became tenants in harmony. After a while, this developed into a full, loving relationship. I spent time at Shenton helping with internal decoration of the billiard room for Father and also at my sister's Georgian farmhouse, spending many weeks helping out with a multitude of tasks with her property business, feeding horses, and anything that needed doing, providing it wasn't too complicated.

For Father's birthday treat, on 1 May 1991, the family clubbed together and arranged for him to have a pleasure flight on the Concorde in July. The reader can imagine, with his wartime fighter pilot exploits, what an immense thrill that was for him, although I don't suppose he was allowed in the cockpit this time.

I made dozens of applications for new jobs over the next few years, but my age and the fact that the construction industry was in the doldrums didn't help. So I turned to helping my partner with the business that she owned, a Health and Beauty Salon for men and women, in Southampton. Unfortunately, due again to the recession and staff problems, my partner's business went into administration during 1992, and we both had to turn to selling products and services by telephone or at local exhibitions, visiting clients homes, and using the cottage as our base.

My partner was a great believer in the spirit world and would occasionally talk to a psychic medium about her life and business opportunities. She introduced such a person from Bournemouth to the cottage one evening, although I was very sceptical about the entire subject. But after listening to what this woman had to say, I recorded a handwritten aide-memoire immediately afterwards, dated 7 November 1992. She spoke to me mostly about my family, and I've kept it all these years.

The medium, named Ann, started by talking about my partner's deceased father and described him perfectly, including some of the clothes he often wore. Through a spirit guide, the medium talked through many aspects of his life, with his daughter listening intently. All I can remember is that Ann described the clothes he used to wear, and he told her that the arthritis in his hands had gotten a lot better.

Here is an extract from my aide memoire written in 1992, with every word recorded as Ann spoke it. I was utterly astonished at her knowledge of my private life. Things that even I had forgotten came through from the spirit world.

Ann started by referring to Mr Ernest Hughes, my adoptive dad. Incidentally, I recall that during his lifetime, he had been a believer in the after-life.

"Dad said that in my twenties I drove a Morris Minor—grey in colour." That is correct. I also wrote, "He told Ann that I would remember being bitten by a Dachshund." That is quite true. It was when I was about 5 years old, on holiday at Lyme Regis, but I had forgotten the incident. "He then told me not to be ashamed of my upbringing." How on earth would Ann know details like that without some guidance from above?

Ann then went on to talk about the spirits in the New Forest cottage we rented, a gamekeeper and a poacher, one of whom was called Roger Reynolds, and Kate the Housekeeper. All were dressed in nineteenth-century clothes, and Ann confirmed they were all friendly. However, after a tour of the cottage, she warned us of the negativity and the strange coldness in one of the bedrooms. She advised that it was not a suitable room to carry on creative work needing concentration.

Later, she described "Great-Grandfather John Hall, wearing plus-fours, with a very smart waistcoat, a monocle, a large moustache—a real country gentleman, who had a special walking stick with a carved lion's head handle." The description matches perfectly John Hall's photograph I have, shown in chapter 23, but I have no knowledge of the walking stick.

Ann then described my natural parent's house. "A large mansion on a hill, with a lake lower down, a trout stream, and a rowing boat." Ann said she was receiving these messages from Marjorie, who described some of the paintings in the house. "A Mona Lisa-type lady, a rather dark painting. A painting of Shenton Lake, in the corner of the drawing room. A ballet dancer in a long dress. Galloping horses, manes flowing."

Marjorie asks, "Did I get the silver?"

"Yes," I said, "two cigarette cases."

Ann says, "Well, Marjorie says you should have had a lot more." Ann continued that Marjorie was "very sorry I had to let you go—her friends at the time thought it wrong. She has spent her life wanting me back, having found me then lost me again, and she will never leave me now."

There is still a half-page of more personal dialogue in my aide memoire that I can't publish. Ann wasn't the only medium that visited the cottage. Many years later, just after Peter Hall died, a horticultural consultant colleague of mine brought his wife, Rita, to the cottage on a social visit to admire the garden, particularly the shrubs. Rita started a conversation with my partner about her interests and explained that she had studied spiritual communication with the other world for most of her adult life, at the Arthur Findlay College of Psychic Science at Stanstead, in Essex.

I had no idea she practiced in this way; her husband had never mentioned it to me. I can still see Rita standing in the doorway of the cottage and saying to us, "There is an exuberant man clamouring to tell me about his exciting flying career and a female voice talking at the same time." Rita halted the session, and then we came inside and sat down. Rita then described both Peter and Marjorie Hall, who were having separate conversations with her about their lives on earth. Rita conveyed their words to me. I had never met Rita before, and I was utterly astounded at her powers of communication. I didn't make any notes after they had gone, so I can't relate what was said in detail, but we were both very astonished at what had occurred.

I did not get a full-time, salaried job until August 1995, at the ripe old age of 59. In the intervening four-year period, with the encouragement of my partner, I trained as a physiotherapist specialising in back pain. We also became involved in marketing a very expensive physiotherapy couch from Germany that vibrated, selling herbal products and proprietary slimming products called Micro-Diet through an American company, marketing a health drink to top athletes, and marketing a fuel-saver device for cars and large goods vehicles. I joined a charity promoting the cochlear implant for deaf people of all ages, sponsored by Esther Rantzen's husband, Desmond Wilcox. As part of our awareness campaign, two of us on the fundraising committee were invited to witness an implant surgical operation at the Southampton General Hospital.

I also travelled to Kent on a weekly basis to join a consortium group of associates: a property agent, an architect, a structural engineer, and a financier. I was staying at a bed and breakfast for several months to assist in promoting a new development company in the United Kingdom. Unfortunately, this folded after we reported our suspicions to the fraud squad of an international money scam operation by individuals that were attempting to fund us.

For a couple of years, the same structural engineer colleague and I prepared designs and drawings for precast, concrete seating terraces at football grounds like Wolverhampton and Swindon. Next, we set up a five year concrete-repair contract, with annual inspections to a multistorey car park for Fareham Borough Council in Hampshire. These projects kept the wolves at bay for a while. When this work ended, life became even more difficult. After eating into our savings, we considered posts for a cook or housekeeper and handyman or for house-sitting empty properties while their wealthy owners were away.

However, we continued to survive at the New Forest cottage until I struck lucky and secured a project management team leader job, with a major multi-million pound turnover contractor, called Amey Facilities Management Ltd. It was a contract for a £6 million internal refurbishment at Ordnance Survey's headquarters on the edge of Southampton. I was awarded this position in August 1995, at the age of 59.

The five-storey offices for map-making and support administration of 2,000 staff, needed new raised floors, new ceilings, special lighting, upgraded electrical supplies, air conditioning, and new communication systems. This had to be done without interruption to the daily working practices of a process that put raw paper in at one end of the complex of buildings and got a range of finished maps out at the other. The refurbishment involved a lot of off-peak hours for all trades, and I was putting in sixty hours each week for nearly eighteen months to finish on time. To implement the stringent health and safety regulations on an hourly basis was a nightmare, and there were staff complaints about noise, dust, and disruption. However, I was working for a fine management company, and this project led on to better things.

After this contract was completed, I was transferred to HMS *Nelson*, a large land-based ship in Portsmouth, as part of a small management team seconded to the Commodore's staff. This involved a unique out-sourcing partnering contract, which, at the time, was the first such contract in the UK between a private contractor and the Ministry of Defence. I worked there as the estates manager, responsible for the upkeep of all premises and the extensive sports facilities, with the equivalent rank of lieutenant commander until I retired in 2001. It was exciting to be back in service life again, particularly at this senior level.

Aerial view of Brian's rented cottage, centre, in the New Forest—1990's

– 19 –

FATHER'S DEATH, 1995

As described in chapter 16, Father and Geddie continued to enjoy all the pleasures of country life at Shenton. However, because of the large gap in their ages, they had a few differences. Other than intermittent visits throughout the years and at Christmas, I did not visit Shenton very often after Marjorie passed away. I had a new relationship to foster as well as keeping the bailiffs from calling and coping with a multitude of different jobs. At the same time, I needed to look after my ailing adoptive mother, who was in her late eighties and showing signs of dementia and other illnesses. She encountered increasing problems in looking after herself. Furthermore, I had to look after the rented cottage, which was falling apart in places, and a huge garden. I sensed that father and Geddie were much entwined, and I felt they needed their privacy. However, it was obvious from Father's letter in October 1994 that his health was deteriorating and reducing his ability to carry on his active social life.

My last visit to Shenton was at Christmas in 1993, and there is no entry in my diary for visits in 1994, not even at Christmas. I kept in regular contact during the year through phone calls and letters. In early February 1995, just before the anniversary of Marjorie's birthday, I phoned Father and was told by Geddie that he was very ill. Although he had hunted during January quite normally, his pain by then had worsened, even with morphine tablets. I made immediate arrangements to drive up the next day. I had known for eight years or so, although he had kept the facts secret from Marjorie, Father had been getting treatment for prostate cancer. His PSA shot up to a very high level in 1994.

During February, I spent six days at Shenton, helping out where I could with looking after Father, doing some repairs to the house, and running errands. He improved a little. My sister, Carolynn, and her husband, David, and other local members of the family were regularly at Shenton to support Geddie and help look after Father.

On 21 February, Father wrote an account of two mating foxes just outside his window, which I quote here.

Who has seen two foxes mating at 5.00 a.m. on a cold, damp winter's morning? Not many of you, I bet, and I did not actually see it, but having witnessed the foreplay, I have a pretty shrewd idea of what happened next!

It is twenty-eight years since I was a master of fox hounds (MFH.), but it had never been my good fortune to see the propagation of the fox species being enacted, without which, fox hunting would surely be terminated more effectively than by any legislation or protests by antis or the effects of financial stringency.

I was confined to bed for what might well be the final curtain and was awoken at about 04.30 a.m. by this incessant barking under my bedroom window. I guessed it was a fox, and this was confirmed shortly afterwards by a mobile, younger MFH, who appeared with a good flashlight and better eyesight.

The beautiful vixen had arrived from the iron gates and sat in the front drive, waiting to be wooed. We could see their bodies vaguely, but their eyes shone out like Christmas tree lights such was their excitement. I hung on for a while, hoping that this young fox could show an old dog a few tricks; but, alas, they disappeared under a bush for the final act.

Peter F. Hall   *21 February 1995*

I spent five days at Shenton, 17-21 March. Father even needed me to help him stagger to the bathroom. It was heartbreaking to watch. His general practitioner called in regularly, and Geddie and the rest of the close, local family were there and wonderfully supportive. Geddie was stoic throughout but close to tears.

After returning to Hampshire, I telephoned on Saturday, 25 March hoping for good news, but Father was very poorly. Geddie told me he could hardly speak; he was in severe pain and had been put on a syringe driver to drip-feed morphine into his lower body. On Tuesday evening, 28 March, I got a telephone call from my sister, Carolynn, recalling the traumatic events of the previous few days. She said that on Saturday, 25 March, Geddie had rung her and said Father was very ill and had been hallucinating badly. His breathing was very poor.

The next day, Sunday, 26 March at 08.00 a.m., Geddie rang Carolynn again and said, "Please come urgently. Your father wants to marry me." Much discussion took place that day regarding the possibility of a death-bed marriage. Clergyman John Plant was consulted, and he then consulted his bishop. Then the GP was asked for advice. After eating jelly and ice cream at midnight, Father was awake and recovering in the early hours.

Carolynn continued, saying that early on Monday, 27 March, Father asked for his usual morning cup of tea, cornflakes, banana, and toast. Solicitors were then consulted about a possible marriage, but they pointed out his will would then be null and void. Any new will could not be signed, due to Father's inability to sign his name at that point. Apparently, my brother Tim hit the roof when he heard about the marriage plans. Following the legal advice, alternative plans were made for a blessing for Father and Geddie as a couple on Tuesday, 28 March.

At Tuesday lunchtime, the Reverend Plant gave Father and Geddie a blessing, in the presence of Neville, Carolynn, and David, whilst they all drank champagne in the morning room's bay window, surrounded by bowls of roses.

My diary states that, whilst I was preparing supper for myself at the cottage in the New Forest that evening, on Tuesday, 28 March, just after my sister had telephoned, I sang, very loudly, for the first time since I was a choir boy, Handel's "O for the Wings of a Dove", with these lyrics. "Far away, far away would I roam, in the wilderness build me a nest, and remain there for ever at rest. In the wilderness build me, build me a nest, and remain there for ever at rest". This poignant but unconscious message, perhaps to my father, was followed by a loud bang, caused by a dud lamp bulb in my bedroom, just before bedtime. My diary note continues that I had a very bad dream that night about Shenton Hall being full of noisy people milling about, and I was aware of an organ playing church music.

The following day at 07.15 a.m. on Wednesday, 29 March, Carolynn phoned me from Shenton to say that Father had passed away in his sleep at midnight, with David, Carolynn, and Geddie by his side.

This was such very sad news, the end of an era. It happened just twenty-four hours after Father and Geddie received their blessing. Sadly, I only knew my natural father for thirteen years. I am pleased that I took the steps to find my natural parents, but I accept that it caused some upset in the family. Members of the family came to terms with the situation at different times.

I set off for Shenton that morning to join my siblings to discuss the funeral arrangements. The prognosis was a tumour on the prostate that had previously erupted around Father's body and was gradually attacking his lungs and then his bone marrow. I spent several days at Shenton with my siblings, all of us consoling one another as best we could. We made the house ready for the reception after the funeral, and amongst shared tears and some hard work, we briefly rejoiced at the news by telephone of the birth of my first grandchild, just four days after Father passed away.

Father's funeral, held in the same church as our mother's, six years earlier, was on Tuesday, 4 April. More than fifty family members were present, and there were dozens more in attendance, including Father's business acquaintances and colleagues from the hunting fraternity and many other friends and staff from the factory in Hinckley. Father had left instructions that I was to be seated in the front pews with the rest of the family, as recognition of being his eldest son. We all went back to Shenton after the funeral service, and Father was laid to rest in the same grave as our mother, at St. John's Church in Shenton, opposite the house they had lived in together for thirty-six years.

Soon after the funeral, I wrote to the Reverend Canon W. E. Quinney, All Saints Rectory, Nailstone, Leicestershire, to thank him sincerely for his inspiring address and requesting, if possible, a written copy, and here is an extract.

My association with the Hall family goes back to my childhood at Stoke Golding when I delivered the newspapers during the war to Oaklands, their family home in Stoke Golding. Peter Hall's father Frank, a paragon of virtue if ever there was such, taught me in the Sunday school and Bible Class there. Some may feel that the faithful seed which he sowed did not fall upon stony ground. A handful here today will know of the circumstances which bring me here today. Many will not.

Some long time before Peter's illness was diagnosed as a terminal illness, we met at Cliff House, Twycross, for a social event. During this occasion when Peter, I recall, made an excellent speech of appreciation for our host's contribution to the life of the Atherstone and beyond, he approached me and said I want you to take my funeral. Well aware of his acerbic repartee and anxious to forestall it, I replied that I was busy for the next two weeks. And anyway, I was the world's worst at dispensing patronage, which he would obviously require in good measure. He quickly retorted that patronage, using another adjective, had been my stock in trade all my life. We continued to sip our soda water. He had a wry sense of humour.

Your presence here speaks more eloquently than these halting words of mine. Your own personal reflections will no doubt enjoin my own largely pointers to a complex character, but one whose strengths and weaknesses reveal a remarkable man.

Time constrains me to chronicle the many activities in which he was involved and of which he excelled. Without doubt he was a capable man, possessed of an agile brain, a perfectionist who did not suffer fools gladly. His early wartime career as a fighter pilot is well known. His Mosquito plane was shot down over Holland, and he was imprisoned in the infamous Stalag Luft III camp, where he helped plan the abortive and now famous escape. Returning home after the war, he rejoined the family hosiery firm Hall and Son, later taking over from his father. With consummate skill, Peter developed the company, knowing personally every employee, and though known as a hard taskmaster, was universally known as being absolutely fair. On hunting days, he was at the factory at 6 a.m., returning there in the evening as often as not. Such was his astuteness that not a few contracts for work, it is said, were secured from difficult representatives by inviting them for a flight in his light aircraft; the suggestion being that he frightened them into submission. On his retirement as president of the Hinckley and District Knitting Association only weeks ago, the secretary said "no one has served the industry in a voluntary capacity with more distinction."

I imagine this could well be said of his occupancy of all the leading positions in the Atherstone Hunt. He lived for hunting and loved shooting and field sports. A deft horseman and successful breeder of them he was show jumping into his 70s and in the hunting field until a few weeks before his death.

Over some fifty years and more, standing faithfully alongside was Marjorie, who with the children provided so much interest and happiness. At one time churchwarden at Stoke Golding, a sidesman at St John's Shenton, where he worshipped regularly. The tradition of the established church related well to his conservative tastes, and he supported both churches.

Peter, as one of his sons remarked, "lived on the edge", requiring adventure and challenge at every turn. You may feel that this was evident in his approach to his terminal illness. My own observations suggest that he did not die unfulfilled. In the fullness of years, tended lovingly by family and a special friend, he passed over to the other side. For him, the tensions of this life are over, and he surely knows God's peace. Peace to the memory of a soul of worth. It has been rightly said that the burial place of good men and women is in the hearts of friends.

This is a wonderful accolade to my father. In addition, with the help of Tim's remarkable memory, I can relate that Father's passion for cars was legendary; in the sixties, he had an Aston Martin Volante, and then an Mk1 Jensen, his favourite car which he kept all his life, together with the original documents.

Over the years, he also had a Lagonda, Daimler Majestic, Jaguar V12 E Type, Humber Super Snipe, Daimler Coupe, and an Alfa Romeo. His last car, a BMW 325i, he kindly bequeathed to me in 1995. Due to his exceptional knowledge and keen interest in engines of all types, he kept meticulous records of petrol, oil, and water used and journeys made for all the vehicles at Shenton Hall.

– 20 –

FATHER'S RAF CAREER, 1938-45

As mentioned in chapter 9, my natural Father joined the RAF Volunteer Reserve in 1938 when he was 22, "More as an adventure rather than patriotic fervour", as he wrote in his eighteen-page, typed memoir, based on his RAF logbook, during September 1980, thirty-five years after World War II had ended. As a tribute to my father's enormous courage and bravery, here is a summary of his memoirs.

My brother-in-law and I decided to present ourselves at Leicester to join the RAF Volunteer Reserve; we just felt it would be fun. Nor did we have any flying connections—he was a farmer's son, and I was just settling into the family business. It provided a modest supplement to my wage of £3.50 a week. An extra one shilling per hour and a penny a mile travelling expenses were a great attraction in those impecunious days; at a time when I was saving up to get married, any extra money was very welcome. The income from the Volunteer Reserve enabled me to buy a Royal Enfield super motorbike, which was later traded in for an Aerial Square Four.

International events looked gloomy, but that was no concern of ours. Any thoughts of the possibility of war were discounted, believing our leaders had the matter in hand. A stiff medical and intelligence test reduced aspiring aviators from forty-three to three of us on that day in November 1938. We spent many evenings and weekends with our training instructors before that magical moment when we were allowed to get airborne, late January 1939.

Conditions were rugged: open cockpit, goggles, and leather helmet, with the instructor sitting behind giving his instructions through a rubber tube, competing with the Tiger Moth engine noise and wind roar, a semi-gale which seemed likely to pluck the skin from one's partially frozen cheeks, and the rest of the body wasn't too warm either. Later I flew solo, after mastering the difficult job of the extraordinary habit of the Tiger Moth bouncing on the runway during landing trials. We were married in April, and after a blissful summer, I had totted up more flying hours on Hawker biplanes.

It was in September 1939 that we heard the fateful announcement that we were at war. We were asked to report to RAF Cambridge with our belongings and prepare for all eventualities. After poignant farewells to new bride and the family, we set off, not knowing whether we should ever return. The RAF had taken over Trinity College for our further education, chiefly in ground duties and marching in proper uniform.

By November 1939, we were considered to know enough about discipline to be allowed back on to flying. We were all RAF sergeants, which was the basis we joined the VR with, the strong hint that commissions would more or less be automatic. A batch of us were posted to Brize Norton to fly a Harvard, a splendid aeroplane, and to live in freezing cold wooden huts. Within three days, I had gone solo and been chosen for special duties to disperse aircraft into fields to avoid enemy bombing raids, then dashed home for weekends on the Ariel motorcycle.

At an interview with my wing commander, I was asked if I would like a commission. I replied I was happy with all my fellow sergeants and would like to stay with them. What I didn't know was that most of them had said "Yes, please". So only Basil Quelch and I were left as sergeants. No matter. We were in it for the flying, not promotion. In April 1940 we were posted to Penrhos camp in North Wales for live firing practice near Pwllheli. Marjorie joined me and we celebrated our first wedding anniversary there. This led to us being given our wings and had a passing out party, which I have little recollection of except being very ill afterwards, more than ever before or since!

Author's Note One: I found yet another coincidence, unbeknown to me at the time. I was also posted to North Wales for my national service training as an 18-year-old soldier and, like Father, lived in a cold wooden hut. I was also there for live firing practice but using twenty-five-pounder artillery shells on a firing range near Trawsfynydd, in what is now called the Snowdonia National Park. It was about twenty miles eastwards from where Father had carried out his firing practice fourteen years earlier. None of my brothers were old enough to be drafted into national service.

Our posting to Aston Down led to us flying fighter Blenheims, although we should have progressed to just Spitfires or Hurricanes. During this time, France was overrun by Germany. This was soon followed by a posting to 235 Squadron Bircham Newton, which was rather traumatic, to replace a crew who had just crash-landed on the airfield the week before, and we had to attend their funeral. The only billet left was number thirteen, but it must have been our lucky number, as Basil and I were the only crew remaining after twelve months. Our first operational trip, on June 25, was in a formation of nine aircraft over Holland. I was petrified, but we saw neither enemy fighters nor anti-aircraft fire. The Air Ministry sent another nine aircraft over the next day, but we weren't included, as we were assessed as too green. Just as well; they ran into trouble, and only two aircraft returned, and we lost our flight commander, "Pissy" Peacock, a daredevil flying type.

Author's Note Two: I have just found the RAF Bircham Newton Memorial Project website, where it confirms Father's account of one of our returning bombers crashing on the airfield landing strip with the loss of three aircrew. According to local legend, the airfield has a string of ghosts from World War II.

Our next mission was to escort convoys going up and down the east coast, flying Blenheims armed with four machine guns. I had a very good navigator and a cryptic air gunner. We left at 03.00 and stayed until relieved, a thrilling experience. By the summer, the

Battle of Britain was hotting up, and we had one or two skirmishes midflight with Fritz, when we spotted a batch of Heinkel III's, one of which we badly damaged by firing all our ammunition but got hit ourselves in the port engine. As we were over Norway, it was a long way to go on one engine, so I decided to head for home. On 22 August I had a slight problem near Le Havre, when I met an obvious German trainer a few miles out to sea. Should I regard the two pilots as potential bombers of London or give them the benefit of the chivalry most pilots extend to each other even when enemies? I will not remember whether I actually shot them or not, but suffice it to say that they flew into the sea when executing violent evasive manoeuvres very low down.

The months continued with flying missions from Bircham Newton near Kings Lynn in Norfolk to St Eval in Cornwall, in all weathers. Looking back, I cannot understand how we managed with minimal radio help to keep to our assignments. My new navigator must have had a transfusion of pigeon blood, and my rear gunner deserved a medal for just being there in such cramped, cold, and dangerous conditions. No praise is too high for the ground crew, many of them butchers or bakers only months before but licked into shape by crusty old flight sergeants who worked all hours to keep our aircraft flying, with repairs to bullet holes and to vital hydraulics and electrical circuits. Throughout all the war, I never had an engine fail due to bad maintenance or damage due to enemy action; it was always diagnosed quickly and put right. I wish I could say the same about the maintenance of my private aircraft now.

The most frightening experience I had was on 16 Dec. 1940, when three Blenheims set off to escort minelayers in the North Sea. At dusk we left the convoy but could not get back to Bircham Newton because of an air raid, so no runway lights. All three of us including our leader, a most experienced pilot, flew back out to sea, circling low down and waiting for the air raid to end. By now we were quite lost, and radio contact was nil, as usual, but we kept closely together, retaining vision of our wingtip lights. Our leader banked steeply to turn, and it got steeper and steeper until I had to break away, only to watch with horror our leader crash into the sea and burst into flames. I did not know what to do or what to say but just flew aimlessly around, horrified. After about two hours, I saw some faint lights below and landed on them to find it was Bircham Newton. A few minutes later, Basil Quelch also landed safely. Truly, the Almighty had Billet 13 under his special care, and after we thanked Him, we repaired to the mess for a whiskey for the first, but not the last, time.

We continued to escort shipping conveys across the Atlantic, based at Aldergrove in Northern Ireland and had accumulated 570 flying hours, most of which were exciting and all of which was educational.

A posting to Catfoss in Yorkshire, after surviving a year of conflict operations, led me to provide operational training for younger and less experienced pilots during my rest period. Basil and I found a house on the coast at Hornsea and brought our wives up for the duration of the posting. Food was short, so we had to supplement the larder with the local game, shot with a .22 rifle. Next posting was to Upavon in Wiltshire, the Central Flying School, the crème de la crème of the Air Force, a military flight training school. My wife joined me, and we decided that as the future looked secure, we should start a family. We must have rung the bell first time because Neville was born in June 1942.

Author's Note Three: I must intervene here again to say that it wasn't quite the first time Father had rung the bell. Father was writing this in 1980, not dreaming that in 1982, his real 'first ring of the bell' was about to knock on his door at Shenton Hall. Another incredible coincidence is that Father's posting to Upavon in Wiltshire, as I have just found out on the map, is about six miles north of Larkhill, which runs alongside the B3086, where, in 1955, I spent six months at the Royal Artillery School for Surveying before being posted to Germany. Again, there was a gap of fourteen years in experiences between father and son. What a shame I couldn't share these amazing coincidences with him.

After my successful spell of instruction at the Central Flying School, I was commissioned as a Pilot Officer and returned to Catfoss to resume my old job to train P/O's and even F/Lt's during which we continued with a mixture of dodgy night flying, aerobatics, and flying blind through fog blankets, although still in a comparative safe haven based in Yorkshire. By 1943 I decided it was my duty to apply for an operational posting at 521 Squadron, back at Birchham Newton in Norfolk. By this time I had flown 750 hours, made up of over 900 flights, and had taught hundreds of pupils. My shooting ability had improved, which would give me a better chance of survival than when I joined in 1940.

I wanted to return for several reasons: the pheasant shooting was better, a new marvellous Mosquito airplane had arrived with a terrific range, four cannons, and so fast it didn't need a rear gunner. What a wonderful opportunity, too good to miss. The first shock I got back at Birchham was 521 had been converted to a metrological squadron, so no heroic stuff shooting down Germans. The public image of a weather squadron was even worse than a PRU (photo reconnaissance unit). The next shock was to see these beautiful Mosquitos were completely unarmed, so all my expertise acquired over the past two years was to be wasted.

In flying terms, back at Bircham was all one could wish for: taking off in a Mosquito, Spitfire, and a Gladiator all in one week. I was blessed with another good navigator, Bill Woodruff, who rose to be top-dog air traffic controller at Heathrow. We had to climb to 25,000 feet every dawn and every dusk, whatever the weather, to measure the cloud heights, temperatures, visibility, and so on. The Spitfires were used for 40,000 feet every midday, obtaining the same information; 40,000 feet is fairly high today and seemed an awful long way up 40 years ago. We didn't always make it but had to keep going up until the aircraft stalled. We had oxygen, but as an additional help, the Spits were pressurised. The Mosquito was a twin-engine Spitfire made of wood, beautiful to handle. Perhaps they would have been less mobile had they been weighed down by four cannons and ammunition as I had expected, and I would willingly have traded a little mobility for some armament, because we were expected to fly in broad daylight to any of the capitals of Europe to check the weather. We were about as vulnerable as a virgin walking down Piccadilly, naked.

At Bircham our commanding officer was Squadron Leader Cunliffe-Lister (son of Lord Swinton), and I was second in command—promoted to flight lieutenant—going up the ladder! We now felt we were doing something vital. We used to get far from home, even to Milan, Geneva, and Paris on one trip, taking photographs as a secondary job. Once, over the Baltic coast, we took a photograph of Peenemunde, the German Army Research Centre, reputed to be where Hitler was manufacturing the unmanned flying bombs to win the war, all useful ammunition for future allied bombing raids.

On Sunday, 9 May 1943, we started out on quite a straight forward mission, just to the Ruhr and back, but unfortunately it was clear blue all the way. No trouble at all until over Den Helder on the way back at 27,000 feet and within twenty minutes of home when we were bounced by four FW 190s. It was impossible to avoid them, but it would have been nice to retaliate . . . We were on the Dutch coastline, and if we could have shot one down, it might have discouraged the rest for long enough to dive into low cloud out at sea . . . In very quick time, both wings and the tail plane were shot away, and there did not seem to be much future in remaining with what was left.

Woodruff seemed to agree and was apparently bending down to undo the exit door under his feet—difficult enough in normal circumstances, but nigh on impossible when gyrating wildly downwards. There was a small hatch over the pilot's head and I opted for that, thinking we would get out quicker separately. What I didn't know at the time, thank goodness, was that Bill was not fumbling for the exit door at all but had been knocked out and was unaware of the urgency of a quick departure. The knowledge might have been fatal for both of us, because I doubt whether there would have been time to get him out even if it was physically possible, and there would have been the problem as to *which of his guardian angels would have nipped down and pulled his rip cord for him.*

I managed to pull mine myself and watched the aircraft getting smaller and smaller as it neared the ground. After what seemed ages, a puff of white parachute indicated that Bill was out. What actually happened was that he regained consciousness to see a hole in the roof and so jumped through it just in time to get the chute opened before he hit the ground. How close he must have been is indicated by the fact that he landed in the same field as the wreckage, despite a westerly near gale that had fortuitously blown us back over land again. Meanwhile, I had been blown several miles inland and was doing my best to become invisible because the victorious FW 190s were flying in close circles round me, and I was extremely anxious as to their intentions. Apparently they were decent types, and I finally landed safely on Dutch soil, all in one piece; and this ends the rather lengthy prologue as to how I came to hear the oft quoted phrase "for you the war is over".

Peter Hall   *4 September 1980*

Author's Note Four, January 2013: My brother Tim's family have just found the following Internet information from the Aviation Safety Network—Wikibase Occurrence 51937.

On 9 May 1943 at 20.15 hours a RAF de Havilland Mosquito FB. MK. IV. Flying from Oakington, Cambridgeshire on Military reconnaissance—piloted by F/O 118.042 Peter Frank Hall RAFVR—POW and P/O 130.847 William Charles Woodruff (obs) RAFVR—POW were shot down by a FW190 near Den Helder, Netherlands. Fatalities 0 / Occupants 2: Airplane damage: Written off (damaged beyond repair).

Author's Note Five, February 2013: Whilst putting the finishing touches to this book, another extraordinary coincidence occurred. An email I just received from my brother Tim's former wife, Moe, and their daughter, Rachel, has said that, under a care for your neighbour scheme on the Isle of Man, they made contact with Geoff, an elderly gentleman of 93, who had a courageous World War II record involved with Spitfires during the Battle of Britain. He is now a keen historian and often searches the Internet. After being told about my father's wartime exploits, Geoff searched for "Aces of the Luftwaffe", logged onto www.luftwaffe.cz/olejnik.html, and found the detailed records and a photograph of the pilot who shot down my father in his unarmed Mosquito on 9 May 1943. His name was Robert Olejnik, and altogether he had forty-two victories of shooting down Allied aircraft.

The German records were correct in every detail: date, time, aircraft identification, and the site of the crash-landing, Den Helder, and two prisoners of war. Although PO W. C. Woodruff, Father's navigator, was mentioned, my father, who piloted the aircraft that fateful day, was not. Until seeing this report, our family had no idea how far-reaching wartime records went.

– 21 –

STALAG LUFT III, 1943

This is a continuation of my father's memoirs, dated 4 September 1980, a further thirteen typed pages which, for reasons of clarity, I have included just the salient paragraphs. He continues the story in May 1943.

The first person I saw after landing was a young Dutch boy, who greeted me in English with "You are in the invasion, yes?" Flattering as it was, I couldn't pretend that one petrified, unarmed RAF officer was an invasion, but they had been waiting for us to attack and drive out the Germans for the past year and were inclined to clutch at any straw.

A few more Dutch people appeared and took over my parachute, and I was led through a field and hidden in a patch of brussel sprouts, with instructions to stay there until fetched. Really, by then I should have been sitting in the mess having a cup of tea before going home to the nice house in Cotterham near Cambridge, where my wife and young son had recently been installed. My main concern was that I was fit and alive, but nobody knew and I could not tell them. It was a nasty shock for which I was completely unprepared. The possibility of being shot down had never really been considered. It was always the other fellow's turn. I had never been to Holland and knew not a single word of Dutch or German, and here I was on a lovely May evening, sitting like an idiot in a patch of Dutch brussel sprouts, scared as hell.

I very soon had to do my invisible trick again, when German soldiers dashed up on motorcycles and searched the area; it is a good job they didn't have a dog. About midnight it got pretty cold, and as all was quiet, I did a wander round to see what could be found.

146

Everywhere was locked except a fowl pen, so I joined the hens for the rest of the night. From dawn until about 7.30 a.m. was spent admiring the efforts of hens laying eggs—it must be quite a strain for them—no wonder they make a clatter when it is all over. Size for size, it is about equivalent to a human being expelling an item twice the size of his head.

Soon somebody started to open the fowl pen door, and I prepared for the worst, but it was an old lady dressed in black (she still was when I saw her again in 1952), and after a look of surprise she shut the door but came back five minutes later with a plate of food and the young boy from the day before. He had a set of overalls with him and asked me to put them on instead of my uniform. This completed, we set off on bicycles down the road; of course, I rode on the left until reminded it should be on the right. This might have been our undoing if the German soldiers we passed had been observant. They seemed to be too busy searching for me in the ditches to notice me on the road.

We continued for a mile or so and then rode into a farmyard, where we transferred to a horse and cart ready and waiting. Prospects seemed to be looking up; I always fancied life on a farm and could easily cope with a few months as a farm labourer until the war was over. We drove down the fields and alongside a dyke until we came to a hole about two feet square. Inside was rather cramped, as there were already two other people there.

It seems that they were Jews who had fled from Poland and had been there months or even years and had been sheltered and fed by this marvellous Dutch family. Only then did I begin to realise the incredible bravery of these people. If any of us had been found, the whole family would probably have been shot, and they were prepared, without hesitation, to add to their problems by taking me in as well. We stayed all daylight hours in the not-very-sanitary conditions inside the hole. After dark, the farmer, despite the curfew, would bring us a bottle of milk and a loaf of bread. One night, he even took us back to the farmhouse for a wash. I was alarmed for the safety of his young wife and children.

One evening, consternation was caused because the Germans—still seeking their "Luft Ganster"—were exploring the dykes, and so we had to move. We were taken to a large field of yellow-coloured rapeseed. All discussions took place in a language, presumably Dutch, which I could not understand, and this was very confusing until, one night, a Dutch Parson appeared who spoke fluent English. I had heard wonderful stories of escape organisations through which English soldiers were passed back to home in a matter of days, and so I asked him if he could hand me to one of them. He came back later to say that they had all recently been caught and shot.

It was becoming increasingly obvious that my chances of getting home were nil, and that until I was caught, my Dutch and Polish friends were in great danger because of my existence in their locality; therefore, I had better make plans to become a prisoner of war. I had considerable reluctance to being shot as a spy, so the first item was to get my uniform back. Luckily, it had been buried, not burnt, and so could be retrieved. I was carrying a fairly valuable gold pocket watch instead of the wristwatch lost in the motorcycle accident some years ago. It was left to me by my grandfather, and I could not see much chance of retaining it if the Germans were so short of gold as to be reputedly digging up dead bodies to get the gold from their teeth! My parson friend agreed to keep it for me, and I gave him my address verbally with a faint hope that I might even see it again.

Several years later, there was a knock on the door at Shenton Hall, and there was the brother of the parson, with my watch! He was most apologetic because the glass was cracked—truly the Dutch are a remarkable people.

A day or so later, I walked off and left the people that helped me, I hoped, to a slightly safer existence. Walking along the road, I came to Middenmeer and made one last effort by offering a barge owner 10,000 guilders to get me across to England—it may not be much now, but was quite a lot then—but he said he could not get by the guards on the coast. Feeling hungry, I went into the hotel Schmitt for a snack and was soon told by the owner, in English, that the local policeman had seen me, and as he was in the pay of the Germans, he would have reported it. Sure enough, he came in a few minutes later and indicated I was to go with him.

We went to his house, and I was given the much-needed opportunity for a wash and shave. Surprising how much it improves ones morale to have a wash and brush up. Before long, a Citroen turned up, and three Luftwaffe people got out. This is it, *I thought, and awaited their entry with some trepidation, but my morale was further boosted when they walked in and gave a smart salute—apparently they were NCOs—but I could not reply, as I had lost my cap. After a perfunctory search, I was put in the Citroen and taken off to the local Luftwaffe station, where I was given another meal but could not eat it, as I had already had a snack with the policeman, and being scared as hell is not the best appetiser.*

In the best war stories, one meets the pilot who shot one down, and all are good pals together, helped by glasses of schnapps. Not so in this case. I was quickly whipped off by train to Amsterdam jail, and I don't think what was happening to me really sank in until I heard the cell door bang to, and I really felt incarcerated. It was cell number 21, and I was not let out for two days. During that time, Sergeant Elbon, purporting to be from the Red Cross, asked some questions, but I think he was a fake. Later, during exercise, I met up with an RAF sergeant who had been picked up recently wearing overalls, not a uniform. His predicament was that unless he could prove his identity, he would be shot as a spy, and if he revealed where his uniform was and who gave him the overalls, a good Dutchman would be shot instead. I never heard what happened but thanked my lucky stars I wasn't in the same boat.

The next morning at 08.00 hours, thirteen of us and five guards left by train via Utrecht, Cologne, and Frankfurt, arriving at Oberzel at 21.15, where I was put in a tiny cell, number 41. This was the information centre, and the cell was very hot, with an electric radiator full on. We were told that if we answered questions satisfactorily, it would be turned off—perspiration was rolling off us, even with just underpants on, and I did not have the sense to fuse the contraption by urinating on it, as did one fellow down the row. If I had thought of it, I should have been scared of electrocuting some vital equipment—mine, not the Germans.

O/Lt Koch was the interrogator, and I was taken to his office and was flabbergasted to see a whole wall covered by RAF quarter-inch maps, showing every RAF station, squadron numbers, and so on for the whole country. He knew much more than I ever would about the RAF. So I had nothing to offer except the traditional name, rank, and number. They then tried the soft treatment; I was moved to a nearby house, to a pleasant room, clean sheets, good food, cigarettes, and so forth; there were even pretty little children playing in the garden. They had already deduced from the wreckage more or less what our mission was but seemed particularly interested in a new torpedo Coastal Command was supposed to have. Fortunately, I was quite ignorant about this, so there was no problem. Perhaps it was a little piece of the jigsaw they needed to complete their intelligence. There was an awkward moment when I was asked what I had lived on and where I had been, between being shot down and captured, and I thought they were a bit naive to accept that I had dug up raw potatoes after dark and milked cows standing in fields—good job they didn't ask for a demonstration!

There was a compound attached to the interrogation centre, and when they had accumulated about forty of us, we were entrained to Zagan after being visited by a genuine Red Cross official, so that I now hoped that my family would hear the good news quite soon. We were allowed to write two letters home. The journey to Stalag Luft III was not comfortable. We were locked in a carriage with hard wooden seats, having had our boots taken away from us, and the only comfortable place to sleep was the luggage rack, and that was hardly a luxury. We were cooped up for eighteen hours without anything to drink and only brown bread to eat, so it was something of a relief to arrive at Zagan. We abandoned what bread was uneaten and were roundly told off by our fellow POWs in the camp, who were short of rations.

*It was a Sunday, and the first sound I heard was the singing of
the Te Deum at the open-air service, which was well attended. It
really brought a lump to my throat to hear this really English sound
again after so much wandering and uncertainty. I was put into
room 7 in hut 109 with Garwell, Cordwell, Mitchell (Rhodesia),
Van Toen, and Sampson, making six. Later we went up to eight.
Life soon settled into a regular routine after the first few days of
dashing around, seeing who we knew and bringing the old Kreigies
up to date with what was happening at home. Every morning at
08.30, we were fetched out onto the square in the middle of the
compound and counted. This could take a long time, as there were
several hundred of us, and cooperation was not our strong point.*

*We objected to getting up at 08.30, but this was soon put right
by everybody altering their watches to 09.30, which seemed more
reasonable—autosuggestion is a wonderful thing. If there had been
an escape, it was necessary to hide the fact as long as possible, and if
there hadn't been one, it was a good idea for somebody to be missing,
so as to keep the goons on the hop. One day, Kommandant Herr
Pieber became very confused and announced with heavy Teutonic
humour, "Sis time ve vill count the legs and divide by two."*

*After "Apell", the early morning roll call, we went back to breakfast,
usually a slice of bread with whatever we could get on it, having
had a mug of well-brewed tea before going out. At lunchtime,
we had thin soup and boiled potatoes, and the evening meal was
usually delicacies from the Red Cross parcels, without which we
should have been very hungry indeed. The big event of the day
was of course the post. My first letter arrived on 27 July 1943,
having been posted on 6 July, which was very quick. Later on,
when communications were damaged, it could take three months,
and then we would get a whole batch together. Sad indeed were
the faces of those who were left out. We were also allowed parcels,
which sometimes arrived, but my best uniform was lost en route,
and I often thought, I wonder who's wearing it now.*

*It was surprising how time was consumed, considering the terrible
boredom and frustration of being confined within a few acres of*

sandy soil and the only view being thousands of coniferous trees outside the wire. It must have been quite a forest once, before these clearings were made for the POW camps. Tree stumps had been left in places, and we could lever these up for firewood. It is difficult to remember exactly what we did from day to day over forty years ago, but fortunately, I was able to salvage a large exercise book, which contains a daily diary and records of every letter received or sent, with dates and a précis of the contents. There was quite a strong religious content in our outlook; most of us had escaped death by a matter of inches or seconds, and it occurred to some of us that we ought to consider what the alternative might have been.

This was, of course, well-fostered by our resident padres, all three of them. They had been captured in various theatres of war and found their captive audience far more attentive than the perhaps bolshie front-line troops they had been trying to convert earlier on. Sunday was the day when we put on a tie and our best clothes for the church service, and I was heavily involved because for one period, we had the Reverend Eric Jones in our room. The most devoted of high churchman, he even got me to confessions and doing penances. I became one of his servers, which meant administering to his needs during the Holy Communion, sometimes with a daily service. Conditions were primitive and mighty cold during the winters. Water is required for the absolution, and I've known it to be brought in warm but frozen solid before the service was over.

During the first winter, I joined the choir, really for the carol services, which were much appreciated by prisoners and Germans alike. I could not sing very well, but there were some excellent choristers who covered up our mistakes. My diary reports that on 25 December 1944, I felt tired after four services. Midnight Church of England Eucharist was attended by 260 people, and then I went onto the Roman Catholic midnight Mass as a spectator. The temperature on Christmas Eve was 17 degrees below zero, Celsius, which is quite a lot of frost. With eight in a room, we would get quite a fug on, but it was chilly to be first out of bed to get the stove going to make tea in the morning. We slept in most of our spare clothes. The climate in Zagan was similar to England, but more so. Being in the centre of a land mass near the borders of Germany and Poland about halfway between Berlin and Breslau, we were a little colder in the winter and warmer in the summer. August 1943, we recorded a temperature of 100.5 Fahrenheit at 23.00 hours. Unlike other ranks, the guards would not allow us officers to go outside the camp in working parties, so escaping was the only chance of seeing the other side of the wire.

It would have been possible to do nothing all day except to turn out for morning and evening Apell and a few minimal domestic chores, but we were young and active, and various organisations sprang up which made it possible to lead a very busy life. Facilities for these activities were mostly provided by the Red Cross, without whose help we should surely have starved both physically and mentally. Everybody was some sort of expert in civilian life, and very soon, lectures were going for the benefit of the ignorant. Reading took up a lot of time, chess even more. Each hut had a chest ladder, whereby you could challenge anybody three places above you. Newcomers started at the bottom, and it was not long before I was near the top, but it was not so easy on the camp ladder. We had many nationalities in the camp, and some of the Poles were hot stuff.

The date of my arrival at Zagan was 23 May 1943, and escapes by various means were normal practice. Only those involved knew the facts, and security was high. On 11 June, we were all called out for a special Apell at 16.00 because of two suspected exits during the day, and a photo check was called to identify the missing. Torrential rain during the afternoon and what was a hot day turned very cold and damp standing out in the open; we did not get back into huts until 22.00. Trouble went on for a week, woken by Gestapo on 17 June at 03.30; they thought we had a ghost; that is, somebody suspected of escaping but actually hiding in the camp. This was often done to cause aggro and abortive searches outside, whereas if somebody had really escaped, it was important to hide the fact, and sometimes a dummy was constructed and carried out on Apell, so that the numbers would be correct, and the escaper would have a good chance of getting away from the district before the balloon went up.

We had an American in our room, Joe Spontak, a really nice chap. He called here to Shenton just a few years ago and took us all out for a super meal in Coventry, and he still keeps in touch by letter. For Americans, 4 July was, of course, their great day, and the events shown in the film, The Great Escape *were fairly accurate about our camp. My diary reads "Yanks commence procession at 08.00 with horse". I think it was a dummy. Most huts had a brew going, made up of fermenting raisins or even potato peelings and a little precious sugar. After a while, it was ready for distilling with an ingenious contraption of vessels and pipes made from Red Cross tins. All this was viewed with considerable disapproval by the goons, and the ingenuity in making the contraption was matched by the skill in dismantling and hiding whenever a 'ferret' appeared. The distilled liquor was almost pure alcohol and dangerous on its own; we used to keep it to lace with watery beer issued by the Germans on Christmas Day. They never understood how their poor beer could have such an exciting effect on their prisoners!*

On 8 September, goons found a tunnel in the Polish block, starting in the wash house. After the usual panic it was blown up, but they overdid it and blew a hole in the roof, much to the amusement of us onlookers. Two notable happenings this month—Italians surrendered, which bought a spate of forecasts the War would be over by Christmas. Early January 1944 saw another escape, and the consequent Apells and searches were not pleasant in a snow blizzard. Electricity was cut off, which meant no water, but we were able to make tea from melted snow. Oil lamps appeared, fuelled by German margarine with make-do wicks, so we were no worse off than the average Eskimo, but we had no wives to share!

The date 24 March 1944 was a red-letter day in more ways than one; the big escape for which we had been preparing all winter was on. Two hundred of us spent the night in block 104, from which a 100-yard tunnel, 30 foot deep, had been dug. The 500 people who had been working on the venture drew lots, and Mitch Hall and I drew 120 and 121. Most of the people had been engaged on the digging and disposing of the sand, but there was a little army of ancillary trades such as tailors for civilian suits, forgers for dummy passports, and chefs for survival food. My job was making maps in Plunkett's team, other people made compasses, and so forth. All this was done with minimum tools and under constant surveillance from the 'ferrets', who could order us out of the hut for a search at any time. It was quite fantastic how all this work went on without detection.

The story and film The Great Escape *has been well-recorded elsewhere. Sufficient to say, only fifty got out, so we were spared the dubious privilege of trying to walk to Czechoslovakia in several inches of snow with about five million home guards and Hitler trying to stop us. It was interesting that the majority of those caught had maps for Czechoslovakia, and the Germans had some crazy idea that we were off there to start a revolution in that occupied but only partially subdued country. They did not realise that RAF officers' main claim to fame was that they could fly aeroplanes and that starting revolutions was not part of the curriculum.*

Life went on much the same for a few days; we even played rugger. On 6 April, we realised why we had been spared the usual consequences other than canteen and theatre closed. News came in that forty-one of the escapers had been shot—this later went up to fifty—reportedly on the direct orders of Hitler. Those who died were the cream of the camp, many of whom had escaped before. The atmosphere had changed since the early days, when escaping was a battle of wits with the guards, with success bringing congratulations if it was a good effort, and once even a bottle of wine from the Kommandant with wishes for better luck next time.

Author's Note Six: Since Father wrote these incredible memoirs, numbers of escapees have emerged in the press. It is now very easy for me to search 'Your Archives' online, which gives information based on the British Court of Enquiry. It says that out of seventy-six escapees, two reached neutral Sweden, and one eventually reached England; fifty were shot on the orders of Hitler, fifteen were returned to Stalag Luft III, and the remainder sent to other POW camps. The Gestapo instigated an unprecedented manhunt, called a 'Grossfahnding'. Father's memoirs continue with the enormous struggle for all internees to survive the bitterly cold winter, with the Russian Army advancing across Poland towards them. Zagan is situated about one hundred miles south-east of Berlin, just inside the Polish border.

Author's Note Seven: Of all the coincidences in this book, the following occurrence is perhaps the most remarkable of all.

In November 2008, a rather wet and bedraggled young woman rang the front doorbell of my youngest brother's bed and breakfast in Ambleside, in the Lake District, and burst into tears. Her car had broken down about five miles away. After tea and cakes, which all visitors in distress are given, and making arrangements for her car, the woman, Myriam, spotted Father's RAF uniform on a stand in the hall and started a conversation about her Dutch mother and family. Tim gave her an account of Father's escapades after he had been forced to parachute into Holland, and Myriam rang her mother to tell her all about it.

Emails between Myriam's mother and Tim followed, with a story of their family's involvement in the resistance to help Allied pilots who had landed in Holland escape; they also told stories that some of her family were imprisoned by the Germans in concentration camps. Myriam's English step-granddad was also an RAF pilot during the war. Only the previous day, her huge family had gathered to celebrate the anniversary of the family's survival from the Germans and exchanged documents, copies of diaries, and letters about their liberation by the Allies.

Myriam's mother sent Tim a link to the Institute of War documentation in Dutch that listed all the Allied aircraft that were shot down during the war in Dutch territory, with maps. Tim managed to translate and locate Father's records, a Mosquito IV 2013, Flight 1409, Flight Officer P. F. Hall, which crashed near Middenmeer on 9 May 1943. This was quite remarkable, considering the number of aircraft shot down.

Of all the doors for Myriam to knock on in Ambleside, Haven Cottage couldn't have been more appropriate!

– 22 –

RETREAT FROM STALAG LUFT III, 1945

This is a summary of the last five handwritten pages of Father's memoirs, dated 4 September 1980, from his POW diary. These pages describe the time when the entire camp was about to be force-marched by their retreating captors westwards, trudging across Germany in the coldest winter for fifty years, ahead of the feared Red Army advancing across Poland. It was a harrowing and ghastly journey.

Early January 1945: Life in the camp going on as usual. Winter well advanced; ground all frozen and has been since early December. Day spent skating or sitting by wood fire from tree stumps dug out of the ground.

Saturday, 20 January 1945: An undercurrent of excitement spread throughout the camp over rumours of the advancing Russian Red Army only 100 miles away, 3 hours in a car. We were instructed to begin preparations for any eventuality: siege preparation, barricades, warmest clothing, food storage, water supplies, and store in tunnel in theatre.

Wednesday, 24 January: Zero day—knowledgeable people said it was too late to be moved. No guards or transport.

Friday, 26 January: Russians thirty to forty miles away.

Saturday, 27 January: Safe for weekend, getting ready for bed at 21.00. Suddenly told to be ready to move in one hour. Chaos, eat all food we could not carry, make improvised sledges and rucksacks, and adjust to packs forty pounds max. Extreme tension until 03.00, then instructed to vacate camp; we were the last block out but 3. Picked up two packs each—tins thrown out. Wonderful to be outside, deep snow, roads frozen, relief! Straggle off to south-sledges discarded already, lovely scenery. Friendly guard. No aeroplanes—too many tanks.

Sunday, 28 January: By daylight crossing autobahn and reached Halban, eighteen km, told we stay here, but on again to Freiwalden—stay for lunch, old woman with hot water. Very cold in street and all very tired. Rumour we were stopping the night, but find our own digs. Bought sledge for cigarettes. On again uphill seven km to Slingersledge, getting dark, cold wind. Halt at large barn by dark, no food but frozen. Two blankets; very cold, forty-degree frost—one big shiver.

Monday, 29 January: All out by 09.00, nice morning—pretty village, lunch at Priebus, snowing all day and reached Nuckau at 19.00—long, straggling, industrial town. All tired and cross. Go down a hill and back again. One hundred twenty lodged in brick factory. Very warm, just over furnaces. Everything thawed and dried out. Nice to have first wash.

Tuesday, 30 January: Day of rest, as future uncertain; patched up sledge. Guards as tired as us. Twenty not yet reported for duty. Good roasting over furnaces.

Wednesday, 31 January: All Americans moved out. Get a chop for soap. Moved into new billets in canteen.

Thursday, 1 February: Moved to Baron von Arnheim's residence, lived in stables and riding school. Found rest of boys and luggage there; have been in workshops and made sledges. Some consternation due to approach of thaw. Saw Countess drive in on sleigh and pair. On the way again at 22.00, very dark, long uphill pull out of town; hard work, with sledges kept on bits of ice in gutter, very cold night. After nine kilometres, snow really finished and had to ditch sledge. Carried what we could. Many halts for ten minutes;

*fall asleep on side of road. Reached a barn at dawn, told we had to
be off again at 11.00 for Glaustein.*

*Friday, 2 February: Only eight miles to Spremburg but longest ever
known. Issued with barley soup and one hour rest before marching
to station to entrain. Going through wood overtaken by Staffs and
men with spades. Reach siding and scramble forty into a truck,
fifty trucks for two thousand men. Too crowded to sleep, untrained
driver!*

*Saturday, 3 February: Train stopped and disembarked for relief
in cemetery, unpleasant sight. No water, hands filthy, dark in
truck. Went through Halle, no air attacks, thank goodness. Act of
providence.*

*Sunday, 4 February: Bypass the town of Bremen and reached
Darmstadt. Four miles to our next camp in drizzle, four hours or
more whilst being searched—then to bed on straw—dry at last. No
beds for a week, and camp slowly gets organised—made a stove,
get spring beds. More Allied aeroplanes in evidence, shot up by
Mosquito. Much the same until early April.*

*Monday, 9 April: Rumours that Bremen being attacked. Move
possible; frantic making of wheeled carts. All on Apell at 15.30,
told to be ready to move at 17.00. Many objections and go-slow
policy adopted. Got away at 22.00. Air raid in progress, and we
turn back to devastated and looted room.*

*Tuesday, 10 April: off again 09.00, nineteen kilometres to Esslingen
to field, everything carried.*

Wednesday, 11 April: Bokel, field near pub.

*Thursday, 12 April: Field out of town; bring own sticks and water.
Greeted by Tempests flying overhead, RAF notices out.*

Friday, 13 April: Stay in field—bad luck because it rained, tent out of blanket. Helped woman sow potatoes, and got eggs for coffee. Civilians promenade the camp.

Saturday, 14 April: Wind changed in night, so tent a wind trap. Talked with Lieutenant Holze about last brew can.

Sunday, 15 April: Usual day march through orchard country, like Cambridgeshire. Acquired spade. Many apples given away. Stopped on bank of Elbe above Hamburg; made shelter from turves.

Monday, 16 April: Ferry over at 11.00, twenty-minute trip, no aircraft.

Tuesday, 17 April: Two days in field, bathing in stream.

Wednesday, 18 April: Visit to farmer's kitchen, coffee for all; evacuated.

Saturday, 21 April: Beat up by Allied Mosquitos, very frightened. Everything wet next morning.

Author's Note Eight: From service records, we know that by mid-April 1945, most men had reached Marlag Nord Camp, near Lubeck, and were eventually liberated by the British Army. The beginning of the forced march that Father and the rest of the inmates had to endure at bayonet point, between Zagan in Poland and Spremburg in Germany, was about sixty miles. This was by far the worst part of the journey; it was on foot, during the coldest winter of the war, with temperatures of minus twenty-five degrees centigrade. They had little food and sometimes slept in open fields or found a barn or shed. Out of thousands that made similar journeys, hundreds died en route from dysentery, frostbite, diphtheria, and hunger. From Spremburg, the prisoners were intermittently transported in cattle trucks, interspersed by more marching, with the added worry that they might be shot by their guards at any time, or accidently bombed by Allied aircraft during this journey of approximately three hundred miles.

It is likely that the route of my father's forced march across Germany, during his trek northwards towards Hamburg and just before they crossed the River Elbe, passed close to my army location in a camp south of Luneburg, where I was stationed ten years later, in 1955. Sadly, I was not aware of this coincidence whilst he was alive.

It is perhaps ironic that my Father, captured and held prisoner-of-war by the Germans, decided after repatriation several years later, to purchase an old country house near to where he had always lived, that had served as a prisoner-of-war camp for members of the German Luftwaffe. Perhaps some pilots he had fought against in the skies over Europe during World War II.

Author's Note Nine: May 2013. Just as my manuscript is about to be published, my brother Tim found the detailed wartime memoirs of Uncle Bernard, the younger brother of my father Peter Hall. I was not aware these existed until now. These have once again demonstrated extraordinary coincidences with my peacetime two year National Service career, as they have also done with my Father. Here is a summary:

In 1939, Uncle Bernard at the age of 20 joined the Royal Artillery under the World War II compulsory conscription Act. He spent six months training at Larkhill on Salisbury Plain, the exact location that I went to in 1955. Like me, a gunner, he took a course in Artillery Surveyorship and was then attached to a similar Field Regiment to mine, deploying 25 pounder guns. Over time we were both promoted through the ranks from bombardier to sergeant. He was transferred to the 12th Field Regiment, R.A. and eventually arrived by sea at Malta as part of a defensive garrison against a possible German invasion. Malta was bombed by the Germans every day for three years causing widespread devastation right across the island and to shipping sheltering in the harbour. 4500 servicemen and 1500 civilians were killed during this period. My uncle was extremely courageous and lucky to survive. In recognition of the bravery and fortitude of the Maltese people, King George VI awarded the George Cross to the entire island.

During the latter part of this onslaught my uncle was transferred to Tobruk in Libya and after successful officer training, was posted to another R.A.

regiment and shipped to southern Italy. From there, commenced a massive and lengthy offensive against the German and Italian armies pushing northwards through Italy, including the famous Battle of Monte Cassino, during 1944. Many months later upon reaching Florence, the war ended and my uncle returned to England.

– 23 –

BRIEF HISTORY OF THE HALL FAMILY ANCESTRY

The Hall Family Coat of Arms

In recent months, during the writing of these chapters, close members of our family have searched the Internet for information about our family earlier than our own existing records that go back to 1270. We discovered that the first wave of Halls followed the Norman Conquest of 1066 and appear to have settled in Lincolnshire that borders Leicestershire. They are believed to be descended from Earl Fitzwilliam. It seems the name Hall stems from the occupation of the person at that time, being derived from the old French term "halle", which refers to a large manor house. People with the name Hall worked for the lord of the manor as a servant or chamberlain. Our research has found that as far back as the fourteenth century, three coat of arms insignia for the Hall family have existed. One that seems particularly appropriate is reprinted here, with the Latin motto, 'Vive ut vivas' which translated is 'Live that you may live forever'. It features the black Talbot hunting dog.

In December 2000, five years after Father died, my brother Neville found a copy of a family omnibus, forty-seven pages long, in Father's files. An absolute gem! It was originally completed in 1935 by William Thomas Hall, a bachelor, one of the sons of Thomas Hall (1852-1920), and later updated by Desmond Hall in 1976, the son of William Thomas Hall's brother, Henry. Both William Thomas Hall and Desmond Hall resided in Park House, Stoke Golding, close to the village of Shenton, although at different times. Thomas Hall features in the 1982 version of the Hall Family Tree, printed in this book.

Here is a short summary of the more important aspects of the Hall history, recorded in the omnibus. The earliest records date back to Robert Atte Hall of Fleckney, about 1270-1338. His name seems to originate from the fact that Robert, a freeman, held some positions in connection with a large estate. He lived "atte" a hall, and our family tree begins with him.

His son, Richard Hall, in the early fourteenth century, was Rector of Knaptoft, followed by his son Richard, who was Curate of Walton in the middle of the fifteenth century. This led to William Hall of Walton, about 1480-1550, and then to Thomas Hall (I), Curate and Farmer of Walton, about 1584-1629. Here is a verbatim extract from the omnibus.

Thomas Hall (I) was buried at Kimcote on 20th May 1629. His Will was proved on 3rd July 1629.

In the Name of God Amen: Anno. Domini 1629. The five and twentieth day of March. I Thomas Hall of Walton in the County of Leicestershire, Clerke, being sick in body but of good and perfect memory, I doe Institute and Ordain to make this my last Will and Testament. I Bequethe my soule into the keeping of Almightie God and trusting in the merits of Jesus Christ that my sinnes are forgiven me, my body to be buried in the churchyard of Kimcote.

Item: as for my worldly goods, the following: first I bequethe to Elizabeth Hall my daughter thirty pounds stirling to be paid to her when she two years next after my decease. I give to Katherine Hall my daughter £30: to sonne Nathaniell Hall £30; and to daughter

Sara £30, within six years next after my decease. To my daughter
Susanna Pope one black white-horned heafar. To Mary Hall my
wife one bedd in the chamber with the furniture and bedding in
the press in the same chamber: in the parlour one coffer with all the
clothes in the coffers and in the cheste. Also my daughter Elizabeth
Hall three pieces of pewter: also to my daughter Sara three pieces
of pewter of the best. Rest of goods unbequeathed, and debts paid,
the legacies performed. And all expenses discharged he gives to John
Hall, his eldest sonne, whom he makes full and sole executor.

Witnesses: John Archer; Robert Loasbey: Richard Hall, John Sturgis
and Thomas Cooke.

(Signed) Thomas Hall   *Will proved at Leicester 3 July 1629*

Yet another extraordinary coincidence within the family tree: Shenton
Hall, which my parents occupied for fifty years, was built in 1629, the
same year the preceding will was proved.

It is thought that Thomas I was the brother of Joseph Hall, Bishop of
Norwich. Their father, John Hall, was the Governor of Ashby Castle and
resided in the Ashby-de-la-Zouch, Loughborough, and Prestwold areas.
John Hall married Winifred Bambridge, a lady of royal descent; she was
the daughter of Thomas Bambridge, the man who during John Hall's
Governorship of Ashby Castle, was the Bailiff of Ashby-de-la-Zouch. This
marriage produced a son, Joseph, who lived from 1574 to 1656 and he was
one of five brothers and also had five sisters. During his life-time, which
started with a strict puritan upbringing, he was a well-known controversial
satirist, moralist and a devotional writer of theology. Whilst known for his
criticism of the Catholic Church, his church politics followed a middle
pathway.

In 1608, Henry, the Prince of Wales, made him one of his chaplains. He
was nominated Dean of Worcester by James I representing the King at
the Synod of Dort, and then appointed Bishop of Exeter in 1627 and
later became Bishop of Norwich in 1641. Bishop Joseph Hall married
Elizabeth Winniff and they had six sons, and two daughters. Those

recorded in our omnibus are, Robert, 1605-1667, Canon of Exeter, from 1629 and Archdeacon of Cornwall, 1633; Joseph, 1607-69, Registrar of Exeter Cathedral; George, 1612-68, Bishop of Chester; Samuel, 1616-74 Sub-dean at Exeter; and Nicholas, Rector at Loughborough.

I have found that during further investigation in the spring of 2013, that during Bishop Joseph Hall's period at Norwich, both the crown and the church turned against the puritan clergy. As a result, he and other leading puritan bishops were brought before the House of Lords to answer charges of high treason. They were imprisoned in the Tower of London for publishing literature said to be an offence against the Statute of Praemunire. Following their conviction they were released after five months and had to forfeit their estates, living in perdition thereafter. A portrait of Bishop Hall hangs in the well-known National Portrait Gallery in London.

It is a remarkable fact that our family descent can be proved by will alone from Thomas I of Walton, who died in 1629, up to Thomas VII, who died in Stoke Golding in 1920.

The Hall yeoman family lived for four hundred years or longer in an area comprising just the villages of Knaptoft, Mowsley, Walton, and Kimcote, in the County of Leicester. My brother Neville didn't know this history at the time he purchased a farm at Knaptoft, but his choice continued the tradition of the Hall family residing at Knaptoft, right up to the present time.

Indeed, one can claim that the Hall family farmed the land of Leicestershire for seven hundred years. They were never large landowners; nevertheless, they represented a solid and comfortable yeoman family. After reading the full version of the omnibus, there seems to be a spectrum of farmers and graziers, a large collection of ardent Church of England clergymen, a school teacher, a highway surveyor, a Baptist preacher, a hosier, a grocer, a butcher, a tax assessor, a senior civil servant, and a civil engineer, all ably supported, no doubt, by wives who bore large families to maintain the family name.

Perhaps one of the saddest records is the family of John Hall, my great-grandfather who started the family hosiery business in 1882 in Stoke Golding. He and his wife, Sarah Elizabeth, had twelve children, and four of them—Alice, 6; Horace, 5; Kate, 4; and Mabel, 1—all died of diphtheria within four months of one another during 1893. A further child, Sidney, aged 1, died in 1884, and during 1900, Stella died aged 1. The remaining six children, four girls and two boys, lived to varying ages from 32 to 91. Frank, my grandfather, survived the longest of those. He carried on the family business from his father, John Hall.

Frank Hall, who died in 1976, and his first wife, Alice, had four children: Vera, then my father, Peter, who succeeded his father in running the family business, and then Doris and Bernard. My siblings say I sound like Uncle Bernard when I laugh but I look like Father.

On a lighter note, upon searching through an enlarged family history tree, (not reprinted here) the name Victor Borge stood out. After searching Wikipedia, it appears that Victor Borge, born Borge Rosenbaum, married Elsie Shilton in 1933, the daughter of Henry Shilton and Beatrice Heyman, who are descended from my great-grandfather's sister, Susan Hall, who lived 1861-1931. Victor Borge was born in Copenhagen on 3 January 1909. His parents were Bernard and Frederikke Rosenbaum, a gifted Jewish family of talented musicians: his father a violinist, his mother a pianist. Victor died aged 91 after a musical-comedy career that took him all over Europe and America. He performed his whimsical humour 60 times a year, even when he was 90 years old, having made countless musical recordings throughout his long and famous career, some with his adult children. He is in the *Guinness Book of Records* for having the longest running one-man show.

Victor Borge was a child prodigy, playing the piano at the age of 2 and giving his first recital at the age of 8. He then took a scholarship at the Royal Danish Academy of Music. The family fled to America to avoid the Nazi regime in Denmark during World War II, and Victor continued his musical career as a concert pianist and stand-up comedian, affectionately known as 'The Clown Prince of Denmark'. He starred in nine films, including one with Frank Sinatra, performed on radio shows with Bing

Crosby, and conducted world-class orchestras across the world throughout his long career.

I have just found two VHS tapes, *The Best of Victor Borge* and *The Sensational Victor Borge* languishing in my bookcase, not realising for the last thirty years that Victor was, for a short time, one of us.

Returning now to 1981, during the initial search for my natural mother, which led me to the village of Sutton Cheney, I have since discovered over the years and from recent visits, the interesting medieval history of the Church of St James, built circa 1300. It is believed, by tradition that, the very famous King Richard III, took mass at the church immediately before the Battle of Bosworth on 22 August 1495. This was one of the famous and last battles for the English crown in the War of the Roses. Indeed, the King and his troops passed close by on the way to the battlefield less than two miles away. It was to be his last mass, as he was slain during the brutal battle. His naked corpse was taken by cart through the gates of Leicester, escorted by the triumphant cavalcade of Henry VII's army.

Inside the church, there is a modern memorial to Richard III, who reigned as the last Plantagenet King of England for only two years. An annual memorial service for Richard III is held on the nearest Sunday to 22 August, both in the church and at the nearby Bosworth Battlefield Heritage and Visitor Centre, which is a major attraction between the tiny villages of Sutton Cheney and Shenton.

In 2007 a controversy arose over the exact location of the Battle of Bosworth, leading to Dadlington, a nearby village, being examined by archaeologists as an alternative site. More recently, the burial place of Richard III in Leicester has been the focus of research. Historical records indicated that he was buried at a Franciscan friary called Greyfriars, a medieval chapel that was destroyed by Henry VIII. However, this was never proven.

Newspaper reports on 13 September 2012 said that archaeologists who were digging up a Council Car Park in Leicester in an attempt to find the Friary and Richard III's lost grave had unearthed a fully intact skeleton, with what appeared to be battle injuries. This skeleton was thought to be the hunchback medieval king, subject to DNA testing. By 16 November 2012, further reports said scientists would try to reconstruct the face of Richard III using a computed tomography scan. This is the first step towards a lifelike digital image, and there are plans to produce a three-dimensional image of the body.

On 4 February 2013, after further extensive research that included a CT scan, carbon-dating analysis, and DNA verification from a distant relative called Michael Ibsen, the archaeologists announced in a national bulletin that the skeleton was indeed that of Richard III. That evening, a ninety-minute national television documentary on Channel 4 reported in considerable detail the highly successful three-year project that set out to find and verify the existence of the burial site and the missing remains of Richard III, this controversial medieval King of England. After much debate, it has been decided that the King's remains will lie in state in Leicester Cathedral under a ledger stone, rather, than as preferred by the Richard III Society, an elaborate sarcophagus. Despite this proposal, there are interested parties in York that consider Richard III's remains should be buried in York Minster.

Bishop Joseph Hall 1574-1656—an engraving by John Payne—1628

Great-Great Grandfather Thomas Hall 1809-1876

Great-Great-Grandmother Charlotte Hall 1822-1897, wife of Thomas Hall

Great-Grandfather John Hall 1854-1923 taken from the Hall & Son
100 year Centenary Booklet—1982

Great-Grandmother Sarah Elizabeth Hall 1853, wife of John Hall

Great-Grandfather John Hall with wife Sarah
and their six surviving children out of twelve.

Grandmother Alice (Frank Hall's first wife) and her four children,
from left, Vera, Bernard, Doris and Peter (my Father) circa 1920

Grandfather Frank Hall 1885-1976 at his wedding to Eileen Crawshaw,
his second wife and Ivy Fox his sister—1954.

FAMILY TREE - 1982

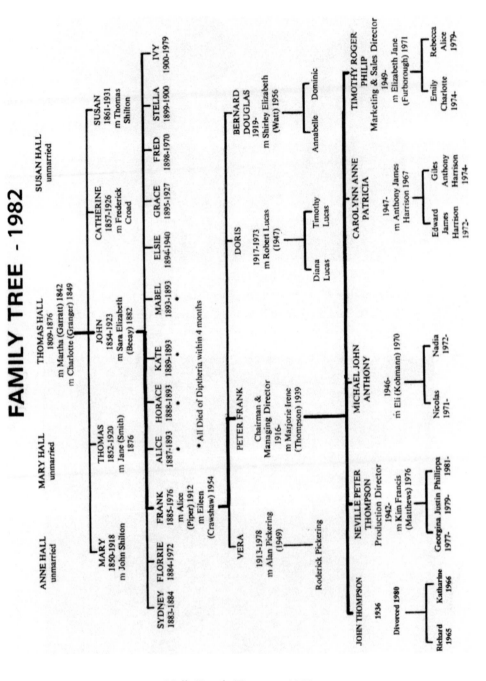

Halls Family Tree as at 1982

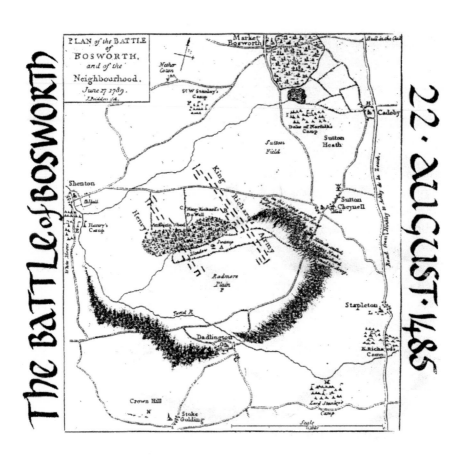

Map of the Bosworth Battle Field 1485, Sutton Cheney

– 24 –

SALE OF SHENTON HALL

My Father, Peter Hall, died in March 1995. Over the next few months, the close family held discussions on how to distribute various items of furniture and Mother and Father's personal possessions between us. Gilding's Fine Art Auctioneers of Market Harborough were engaged to draw up a schedule of the remaining antique furniture, paintings, and other effects, for a sale on the premises on Thursday, 18 July 1996. In the first catalogue were 490 items listed for Part I alone. The proceeds of the sale of the catalogues were given to the Red Cross in recognition of their support for POWs during World War II.

During the late afternoon of the sale, my brother Tim met two gentlemen in the village tea rooms, who had been to the contents sale and said what a fine country house they had just visited. They said they had noticed a well-dressed lady in blue, sitting in the drawing room as they left. Tim was astonished by this, as when he let the two gentlemen out of the front door, there was nobody left in the house. Tim later concluded that it had been Mother having a last look round before her spirit finally left the house to someone else.

None of the remaining family wished to purchase Shenton Hall, as we all realised the large maintenance and running costs would be prohibitive. A variety of national estate agents were approached, and three were asked for a valuation and recommendations for a comprehensive sale of the house and grounds: Strutt and Parker, Savills, and Knight Frank and Rutley, the latter of which the family eventually chose to act on our behalf.

The property took a long time to sell, but a retired American couple eventually purchased it. They spent a small fortune on a major refurbishment that transformed the internal structure but maintained the external facade and landscaped surrounds. I returned to my cottage in the

New Forest and continued regular contact with my siblings and their host of offspring, too many to mention.

During the early 1990s, another coincidence occurred whilst I was living in the New Forest cottage. During the time I was out of work but seeking income via network marketing, I was invited to a meeting in Southampton about vehicle fuel savers. During a conversation with the organiser, Tony Clarke, we talked about our Midlands background and discovered, after ten minutes, that he jointly shared the ownership of Titian Lady, a Ketch-rigged (two-mast) Freedom 40 sailing boat. It had been built by my sister's ex-husband, Anthony Harrison. He and Tony sailed together, sometimes with my sister's sons, Edward and Giles. How amazing was that?

Tony and I have been good friends ever since, and I've joined him occasionally on the boat when it was moored on the River Hamble. He later met and married Pat Robinson, née Jackson, who, as a child, lived in a hamlet in Leicestershire near Shenton, where she grew up with my brothers and sister as playmates. She of course knew my parents extremely well about thirty-five years before I did. This was another amazing coincidence.

I recall a wonderful skiing holiday I took with Tony and Pat and their friends at Breuil Cervinia, in the Italian Alps, halfway between Geneva and Torino. The weather and snow quality was perfect, enabling us to get as high as 9,000 feet, close to the Swiss border.

Tony Clarke and Brian on the Solent in 'Titian Lady'—2000

– 25 –

TRAGEDY IN AFRICA

I devote this chapter to the memory of my nephew Edward Harrison, my sister's eldest son, who was tragically killed on safari in Africa in August 2000. He was aged 28. He had already achieved much in his brief life, and his untimely death curtailed the promise of future achievements and shocked the whole family.

Edward lived life to the full. He was educated at Uppingham School. As well as achieving academic success and entry to St John's College, Cambridge, he was a school prefect and head of house and played rugby union for the First XV. At Cambridge University, he read engineering, graduating in 1995, won a Half Blue in rugby league, representing the University against Oxford University in 1995, and played rugby union for the College. He also found time to participate in the activities of the Cambridge University Officers' Training Corps (CUOTC) and enjoyed an exceptionally varied social life.

After graduation, Edward joined CarnaudMetalBox Engineering Limited (CMB), who had sponsored him at University, as an engineer in their factory at Carnoustie, in Scotland. In July 1996, CMB granted him a sabbatical of twelve months to allow him to take part in the BT Global Challenge. This Round the World yacht race against the prevailing winds takes place every four years. In 1996/97, twelve identical yachts, crewed by amateurs with professional skippers, participated in the race. Edward was appointed as a watch leader on one of the yachts, *Concert*, and they set off from Southampton in September. The boat proved to be competitive with the rest of the field until, when challenging for the lead in the Southern Ocean, *Concert* was dismasted. The crew managed to stabilise the boat and bring her safely home, over 2,000 miles, to Wellington, New Zealand, spending New Year's Eve in the Chatham Islands. A new mast was flown out from the United Kingdom and fitted in Wellington, and the boat rejoined the rest of the fleet in the next leg of the race. Edward stayed with the boat until she finally reached Southampton in July 1997.

On his return, Edward worked at the CMB factory in Carlisle; but, in the summer of 1999, he came to the conclusion that if he was to progress further, he needed to secure additional business qualifications. He was accepted by INSEAD to study for an MBA in Paris commencing in August 2000 and decided, in the meantime, to embark on a belated gap year. He spent the early part of 2000 as a resort manager for a ski company in the French Alps and decided, subsequently, to join a CUOTC overland expedition to South Africa. This expedition was organised to commemorate the centenary of the outstanding achievements of the Cambridge University Rifle Regiment in the Boer War.

The expedition, comprising a party of 32, departed from Cambridge in their Land Rovers in mid-July and progressed steadily through Europe, the Middle East, and down through the North East countries of Africa until they reached Kenya. In Kenya, a break had been planned to allow the party some rest and the opportunity to enjoy a safari before completing the journey to South Africa.

Edward was a keen photographer. One day he headed out from the safety of the compound into the bush in the Masai Mara Game Park at dawn in order to take advantage of the excellent light conditions for photographing the spectacular scenery and wildlife. At around 6.00 a.m. on 20 August 2000, the chief game warden said he was alerted by the persistent roaring of an elephant and left the compound to investigate. Some 500 yards from the camp, he found the tracks of a rogue elephant and the body of Edward Harrison, who had been trampled to death. Edward's body was repatriated to the United Kingdom, and his funeral, held in the same Warwickshire church in which he had been christened, was attended by over 300 friends and relations.

His death at the age of 28 had a profound impact on his friends and family. There was massive national publicity and, for many of his friends, this was the first time they had encountered the loss of a close contemporary. For his mother, my sister, Carolynn, the loss of her eldest son in such circumstances was particularly traumatic. While she has come to terms with his death, she will always continue to mourn for Edward. The tragedy inevitably plunged the family into a period of grief, and I relived the distressing memory of having found, loved, and lost my natural mother over seven years.

Edward Harrison on the BT Global Challenge yacht 'Concert'—1997

– 26 –

CALMER WATERS

Whilst the various shocks and family traumas in my life were spread out and managed over several decades, to condense them into twelve months of writing this, my first book, has exhausted every emotion in me. It has been an incredible journey and a cathartic experience. Now that it is finished, I feel enormous relief. I wrote it partly for my family and partly to encourage other adopted persons to trace their natural parents. In trying to think back over thirty years, I have found the best time to recall and compose the events of my life in readiness for the book is within the early hours, from 03.00 a.m. to 05.00 a.m., but this plays havoc with one's sleep.

It is with some regret that it has taken so long to write this autobiography due to a very busy business life and an equally busy retirement.

I had three specific strokes of luck in the early stages of the search for my natural mother, and I have also counted at least eight very unusual coincidences throughout the book. The irony of the situation is, if my first wife and I had not divorced or, heaven forbid, had she been killed in her awful car crash in 1969, I might never have found out about my adoption. My adoptive parents could have taken the secret to their graves, and even if I had found the adoption papers after my adoptive mother died in 2002, it would have been far too late to find my natural parents. Both had died well before this date. It would have been a very hard job to find brothers and a sister that I didn't know I had—damn nigh impossible. By this time, the verger living at Sutton Cheney, who gave me such valuable information, may have already died too.

The loss of parents is hard for any of us to come to terms with, but to find one's natural parents for only a relatively short time is also very hard to bear. Nevertheless, I am delighted to say I managed to find them, and the three of us were able to enjoy some lovely holidays and weekends together, which, before I arrived, they had not done together for many years. I also found a lovely sister and three great brothers, not to mention their respective wives and husband, many of their grown-up children, young grandchildren, and many cousins, all of whom have enriched my life. I am indebted to my new family for their continuing love and support all these years.

Neville is happily married to Kim, with three grown-up children and four grandchildren. My other two brothers and I have all remarried recently. Michael married Jeab in Thailand in March 2012. He has two grown-up, married children and four grandchildren living in Norway, and 3-year-old twin boys in Thailand. My sister is happily married to David with one son, a stepson, and three grandchildren. As described in the previous chapter, her eldest son, Edward, died tragically in Africa in August 2000. This is an enormous loss for any loving parent to bear. Tim and Lindsey, who married in 2011, during which I played the piano for an hour, now run an award-winning boutique bed and breakfast in the Lake District and have six grown-up children between them.

Finally, I am very happily married to Jill and have two grown-up children and four grandchildren by my first marriage.

Having paused in calmer waters and considered what I have written, it strikes me that running through the entire length of this book is a theme of emotional and sometimes complicated 'threesomes', interwoven by the passion of love.

I have never been a great cat lover; I am rather a dog person, really; my first wife and I had a Labrador retriever when the children were small. We had normal cats but nothing special. My present wife loves cats, always has done, and many years ago, brought up two lovely kittens that, sadly, died 6 years ago, both 17 years old. After our few years together, I was persuaded to visit the local cat rescue centre just to have a look round. We came away with two 10-week-old delightful kittens.

One we named Georgie, who has taken a passionate liking to me. The other is called Bess, and she loves my wife. I have never known a cat to be so affectionate; Georgie follows me around, comes when I whistle, sits on my lap or desk, and purrs like an engine for ages. I'm very puzzled by her behaviour, but I have come to the conclusion that Marjorie has sent her to me.

John with Georgie—2013

Lightning Source UK Ltd.
Milton Keynes UK
UKOW051544240613

212744UK00003B/25/P